———— KEYS ————
TO LOVE

Believing God For A Spouse

EVELYN JAGPAT, PSY.D.

THRIVING MINDS INSTITUTE
AUSTIN, TEXAS

Copyright © 2021 Evelyn Jagpat O'Halloran (aka Evelyn Jagpat)

All rights reserved. No portion of this book may be reproduced, stored in a retrieval system, or transmitted in any form or by any means—electronic, mechanical, photocopy, recording, scanning, or other—except for brief quotations and references in critical reviews, articles, or books, without the prior permission of the author or publisher.

Drevejagpat@gmail.com

Cover copyright © 2021 by Evelyn Jagpat O'Halloran (aka Evelyn Jagpat)

Scripture quotations are taken from the Holy Bible—

King James Version (KJV), copyright 2009 by Zondervan. Used by permission. All rights reserved.

New Revised Standard Version (NRSV), copyright, 1989, by the Division of Christian Education of the National Council of the Churches of Christ in the U.S.A. Used by permission. All rights reserved.

Keys To Love—How To Place God's Love At The Center Of Love and Relationships

ISBN 978-0-9896391-1-8 (paperback)

© Copyright Evelyn Jagpat O'Halloran (aka Evelyn Jagpat), 2020

Thriving Minds Institute

www.EvelynJagpat.com

CONTENTS

Introduction	V
Day 1: Overcome Heartbreak	1
Day 2: No Value	8
Day 3: New Identity—New Nature	15
Day 4: Looking for Love—Searching for Someone to Love Me	22
Day 5: The Gift of Love	28
Day 6: Patience in Love—Waiting for God's Best	34
Day 7: Waiting—Part Two	40
Day 8: Lessons in Exercising Patience	45
Day 9: Great Expectations: Saying Thank You When God Sends the Unexpected	51
Day 10: Hunger for Love	57
Day 11: Waiting in Gratitude	66
Day 12: Your Thought Life	73
Day 13: My Best Friend, Jesus	81
Day 14: Praying in Faith	87
Day 15: Depending on the Source of My Faith	97
Day 16: Spiritual Wisdom	100
Day 17: Willingness to Change	105
Day 18: Dealing with Breakups	110
Day 19: Praying in Faith to Move Forward	117

Day 20: God Is Love — 122
Day 21: God Is Generous — 130
Day 22: Faith = 100 Percent Guaranteed — 133
Day 23: Black Holes Exist — 140
Day 24: Jesus Is My Hole Filler — 145
Day 25: Temptation — 152
Day 26: Spirit of Life Not Death — 157
Day 27: The Promises of God — 165
Day 28: Guard Your Beliefs — 177
Day 29: Love: Core Belief Number One — 184
Day 30: Grace: Core Belief Number Two — 189
Day 31: I Believe God — 194
Day 32: Following the Will of God — 200
Day 33: Faith in Action: Resting in Jesus — 210
Day 34: Scavenger Hunt for Love — 222
Day 35: Learning to Love — 226

About the Author — 233

INTRODUCTION

The truth is, what each person needs and wants most of all in this world is love. Everyone needs love in order to feel worthy, healed, complete, satisfied, fulfilled, whole, and secure. We also need to receive love in order to love ourselves and others, and to develop a stable and permanent sense of identity, worth, and value. The experience of being genuinely loved and of connecting with others in love is a fundamental and essential component of being deeply human. The desire to be loved and seeking to connect in love motivate and influence our behaviors and experiences. This difficult journey of being a woman or a man in the world can never be accomplished without love. We will perish, each alone in despair, if we do not experience love. Neither can your soul and heart feel truly healed and whole without being loved by another unconditionally and completely as you are, for who you are. We each want to be loved with constancy, faithfulness, compassion, and acceptance over the course of our entire life.

On this journey of life, we all seek love to comfort the pain of loneliness and rejection, and heal the wounds of suffering from a broken heart. It is natural to seek a relationship with a partner to satisfy you and make you feel good enough. To fill the void and emptiness and feel less lonely and unloved, we each hunger and thirst for love from someone else. We want someone special, who will value, respect, and love us, and whom we can also value, respect, and love reciprocally. It is essential to our survival as human beings. Yet, the intensely felt need for love often tempts us to compromise and settle for less than what will truly satisfy or make us feel worthy, complete, satisfied, fulfilled, and secure. It is very common to compromise ourselves and values, and give in to desire, lust, need, and less than love, because we are so thirsty and hungry for love. We are challenged in that our desire and need for love is real, and love is really the answer. However, each compromise leads to so much more hurt and a deeper loss of a sense of value, integrity, worth, and self-respect. It also leads to self-condemnation and self-punishment. A pattern of negative behaviors, emotions, and relationship patterns may likely develop, which sabotage your desire to experience quality love and seem difficult to change. The end result is that one tends to compromise even more, and the cycle is repeated, resulting in deeper hurt and an intensified desire for love.

In truth, what you and everyone truly crave and thirst for most of all is perfect love. In reality, it is the only deeply satisfying love that will be able to accomplish what you need it to. However, the ability to love another perfectly can never be achieved by any man or woman in this world. It is impossible for any human being to love another human being perfectly. Of course, it therefore only makes sense that we are really only able to receive perfect love from the source of perfect love, God. God's love is the only solution that makes perfect sense. God is described as being love and love itself is of God (1 John 4:7–8). This means that God is love itself and the source of love. Being the source of love, only His love is perfect and complete. Therefore, it is only through experiencing the perfect love of God that you can feel worthy, complete, healed, satisfied, fulfilled, whole, and secure. It is only through intimately experiencing His compassionate, merciful, and faithful perfect love in a real relationship with Him that you are able to feel unconditionally loved, forgiven, accepted, worthy, valued and good enough, and are able to break the harmful cycle of negative relationship patterns, emotions, and behaviors.

Yet, the love of a human mate is essential. You need a human partner and mate to love you and to love. You need a human partner to share your journey through life with. It is an acknowledged part of being deeply human. The genuine experience of receiving the love of a mate and engaging in reciprocally loving a mate leads to a richer and fuller life. It is also an important part of not feeling alone in the world. However, it is not intended that you attain your value and identity or feel whole and complete through your connection with each other. You may want the perfect human mate to accomplish making you feel valued, fulfilled, and completely satisfied. However, you can expect to be disappointed, because a human mate is destined to fail at doing that job sufficiently. It is impossible for you and your mate to love each other perfectly. You cannot satisfy each other's needs.

When it comes to love, you must honor the characteristics of being both spiritual and human. Both aspects of the self exist, and the qualities of both must be preserved. The needs of both must be fulfilled and satisfied in the way God intended. You need a spiritual relationship with God and His perfect love to feel perfectly loved, compassionately cared for, worthy, valued, whole, healed, complete, fulfilled, and secure. Only God's love can heal your broken heart and help you integrate a healthy identity and love of self. You also need to experience and integrate the love of your Savior, Christ Jesus. In Him and through Him, you have received your righteous identity and grace. Further, you also need a loving relationship with a human mate for a richer and fuller experience of self and life in general, as well as to be connected to another human being by love, as you journey through this life. Life as a human being is never complete without being able to experience love mutually with another human soul. The benefit of this intimate connection and bond with a mate leads to an even richer experience of human love. Yet, the love of a human mate cannot be a substitute for the love of God and Jesus. It does not qualify as being able to satisfy your need for love.

As an individual, you must learn how to integrate both aspects of self and not engage in a constant war between the two. You must learn to better value, respect, and appreciate both aspects of self and the benefits of each, without compromising. When both aspects of self are joined in harmony, you will develop in the area of love. You will also learn how to integrate being fully spiritual and deeply human at the same time, without falling victim to compromising in love and negative, self-destructive patterns and habits. It is the only path to peace and joy in love and life in general. It is the only way you can experience the hope of real love, which satisfies both aspects of self. You can then also experience love for self and others more deeply.

The only way you will experience healing, fulfillment, and completion as a human being and engage more deeply in enjoyment of a quality life is to experience and enjoy the benefits of God's perfect love. To accomplish this, you must learn how to establish a closer and more intimately personal relationship with

God and your Lord and Savior, His Son, Christ Jesus. The quality of their perfect love provides everything you desperately thirst and hunger for. Recognize, however, that to integrate both aspects of yourself successfully, your journey through life requires that you learn how to be intentional about your beliefs and how to put them in practical operation so that they positively impact your sense of self, behaviors, emotions, life in general, and relationships.

The purpose of this book is to give you a concrete and practical way to intentionally practice your faith. It offers practical solutions to help you integrate your spirit, body, mind, and soul, as well as your emotional and interpersonal spheres of being. The goal is to help you integrate both your spiritual and physical natures so that they can coexist in peace and you can function in the way God wills for your life, as a loved child of God. This book is specially geared toward helping you to experience feeling deeply and perfectly loved in your spiritual relationship with God and Jesus. It also offers you a way to apply practical, spiritual solutions which will help you to break old patterns of unhealthy behaviors and ultimately lead to being better able to love yourself and another more deeply and genuinely, in a loving committed relationship with a mate. It offers hope for a new alternative of living passionately in the truth of God's Word, as you learn to integrate both your spiritual and physical natures in peace. As you journey through this book, you will learn how to develop and more deeply experience a real and more spiritually mature relationship with God and Jesus. You will also develop a real sense of your true identity, value, and worthiness, which are constant and unshakable, in Christ.

Additionally, you will learn how to flow in the love and grace of God in your everyday life, especially in the areas of love and relationships. You will learn how to wait for the right mate and how to develop a more mature, loving relationship with your future mate, without repeatedly self-sabotaging, engaging in unhealthy patterns, and compromising your values. Further, this book focuses on how to approach challenges, follow the will of God, and engage in practical, spiritual warfare in the area of love. The practical solutions offered in this book are all based on the Word of God and scriptures are quoted throughout this book.

Further, you will learn how to not compromise in love or be manipulated by feelings of unworthiness, condemnation, desire, need, painful past experiences, and temptation in love and relationships. You will learn how to be in control and command of your thoughts, behaviors, and actions in everyday life and specifically in the areas of love and relationships, based on your relationship with God and Christ Jesus and faith. Benefit from knowing how to live your life based on your beliefs, faith in God, the quality love He alone can provide, and His Word. Benefit from knowing how to more fully walk in the grace of God and let go of endless self-effort and striving. Learn how to actively exercise faith in your life and patiently wait for true love with the right partner. Learn how to passionately engage in life and love again, based on God's Word, without compromising. Learn practical strategies, which harmoniously integrate both your spiritual and physical natures, so that your spiritual nature takes the lead in helping you to navigate this difficult and complex journey through life—of experiencing true love with a partner and mate who God intends for you, and who will love you and whom you will love, the way God wants you to love one another.

KEYS TO LOVE

The Spirit itself beareth witness with our spirit, that we are the children of God...heirs of God, and joint-heirs with Christ ...For I reckon that the sufferings of this present time are not worthy to be compared with the glory which shall be revealed in us.
—Romans 8:16-18 (KJV)

For I am persuaded, that neither death, nor life, nor angles, nor principalities, nor powers, nor things present, nor things to come, Nor height, nor depth, nor any other creature, shall be able to separate us from the love of God, which is in Christ Jesus our Lord.
—Romans 8:38-39 (KJV)

A new commandment I give unto you, That ye love one another; as I have loved you, that ye also love one another.
—John 13:34 (KJV)

DAY 1

OVERCOME HEARTBREAK

Sometimes, in reality, it can be difficult to get through the desire, disappointment, emptiness, and anxiety of not having someone special to appreciate, accept, and love you. This is a very special person who loves you for you and who you love. We all want to receive love, but waiting for the right person or even holding on to hope that he will come can be difficult to sustain or to do alone, especially after hurt and disappointment, or watching everyone else around you with someone special. This is often too difficult for most of us and something which is beyond your human capacity to do without God.

Feeling lonely and desiring someone special to help you feel less lonely, cared for, valued, and to provide you with a sense of validation, identity, purpose, meaning, security, safety, and self-worth can feel like an experience that drowns you in despair. Everything inside of you screams out for relief. It is an agony like no other—to feel isolated, alone, and not loved by someone special. Something inside of you breaks. In this situation, like most of us, you may have at some point reached for love from the wrong person, hopeful that it would satisfy you and offer the safety, validation, and connection you needed. Perhaps you compromised yourself in some way, did something you are not proud of, or even dismissed wisdom, evidence to the contrary, or your own values to attract, win, or attain love. Perhaps you pursued someone you shouldn't have or accepted the attention of someone and settled for less than you deserved. Maybe you even hurt someone else in the process and caused him pain and suffering. Perhaps you acted against good judgment and character. Unfortunately, this is all difficult to see when reason is overshadowed by need, desire, and an intense craving to be loved.

Did I also mention how brutally painful it is to sleep alone at night feeling lonely and unloved? Yes, it is a terrible dilemma to feel like you have to choose between something that may not be best for you or just plain bad for you, and the emptiness of not having a relationship with someone special, who you hoped could make you feel special, fulfilled, cared for, and not so lonely anymore.

After compromising and acting against your character and integrity, you may suffer a further loss of self-respect, which makes the craving to be loved even more intensely painful. It is a vicious cycle. Despite your best efforts, the result will likely be disappointing, and end in a very sad story. You will likely feel less worthy and more unfulfilled, accompanied by a sense of shame and guilt. Invariably, after the cycle repeats in subsequent relationships, you suffer more sadness and disappointment. You may eventually experience disillusionment and crippling hopelessness. You may also fear that no one can ever truly love you for you or want the real you. This may lead you to make even more compromises to maintain connections with others out of need or to at least have something that resembles love, even if it is a lie. You settle and compromise for less. As a result, you feel empty, unworthy, and unfulfilled.

After repeated disappointments and exhausted, fruitless efforts, you may even give up hope of ever being loved, wanted, respected, accepted, and cared for by someone special, who you also have those special feelings for. Eventually, you may feel like your heart just can't take another wound or what, in reality, really feels like a death blow to your spirit. It feels harder to survive. You feel less capable. In truth, you probably feel like you can't stand it anymore. People definitely need air, water, and food to survive, but if you have ever experienced this kind of pain, you also know that you cannot possibly survive without love. Love powerfully connects to everything else, including feeling fulfilled, capable, worthy, and able to achieve purposeful goals in life.

I don't have to imagine the agony because I have personally lived it. It is a pain that makes you want to retreat and give up on life, happiness, and hope. Nothing good seems possible, and every day brings fresh pain and a sense of loss and disappointment. You fade away gradually from your own life, often without realizing it, until it feels like it is too late. This sinking feeling can cause you to further compromise and settle, to do things which are not good for you, and, in the end, give up altogether.

In frustration and despair, you may ask yourself, as I have, "Why does this keep happening to me? Why am I unable to find fulfillment and accomplish meaningful goals in life? Is it that maybe I'm not meant to be loved, fulfilled, and to have a husband in my life who truly loves me?" You may ponder without any real clarity, "Is there a reason why I keep having these repeated experiences of failed marriages, relationships, and goals? Why me, God? Is this just punishment for things I have done?" In discouragement or a desperate need to understand and make sense of your life you may reason that this is your fate or exactly what you deserve as a consequence of your bad decisions, mistakes, ways in which you hurt someone else, did wrong and messed up, or how someone hurt you. You may blame yourself for your own ill-fated destiny.

It is also possible that you may feel victimized and badly wounded by someone else who hurt you so deeply that you can't imagine ever being able to recover and be normal or capable of having a fulfilling life with someone else. Perhaps your past pain established a conflict within—between wanting to be close to someone but being too afraid to truly let your guard down and trust. Perhaps being trusting and open make you feel too vulnerable to anticipated hurt because of how others hurt you in the past. Maybe you just don't see yourself as very valuable and worthy anymore because of what you have done or how others treated you and made you feel. As a result, you may not recognize yourself as being truly special, good enough, and worthy of love.

Often, your past experiences of love, especially in your relationships with family and intimate others, shape your expectations and hopes when it comes to relationships and love. Frequently, the pain of your past relationships will continue to manifest in subsequent relationships, producing a confirmation of having to settle for less than real love or a fear of intimacy. You may find you are attracted to people who eventually turn out to hurt you in similar ways to how you were hurt before. Your negative past relationship experiences often contribute to a pattern of being self-protective and defensive in relationships with others to protect yourself and your heart from being wounded again. You may also feel unworthy and not good enough to be loved.

So, how do you tune into hope and stop doing self-destructive or self-defeating things that harm you again and again? One necessary first step is to accept that your past does not prevent you from experiencing satisfying and healthy love. That system of defensive, self-protective rules you established to keep yourself safe or to secure love and connection with others is hurting you. In reality, it was based on past relationships which failed to offer you love in a healthy and validating way. The good news is that your relationship with Christ disqualifies the past and others from having a stronghold in your life. Jesus died to free us all from sin and to provide us with a new identity and a new way of experiencing ourselves. In Him, we have righteousness. Yes! We are the righteousness of God in Christ Jesus (2 Corinthians 5:21). This is righteousness you receive by faith (Romans 4:3–5).

It means that no matter what happened in the past or whomever may have harmed you and made you feel ashamed, guilty, and compromised in some way, or no matter what you have done, it does not matter. Through your belief by faith, you have received Christ Jesus' righteousness and His identity.

It is by God's grace that you are also a joint heir with Christ and joined forever with Him through faith (Romans 8:15–17). As He (Christ) is, so are you in this world. You have His righteous identity. Not only this, but no matter what you have done or will do in the future, this righteous identity remains yours. Now for more wonderful news! You are loved by God to the same degree and on the same level as Jesus is loved by God (John 17:23). Jesus even prayed that those who came to believe in Him would also understand how much they are loved, valued, and cared for by God (John 17). He wanted you to be focused on how much you are loved by God as His precious child. This position as God's child, which you have received as a believer, comes from Jesus and through His obedience and sacrifice on the cross (Romans 8:15-16). You don't have to earn it. You are now reconciled with God through Christ Jesus as a child of God. This is your righteous position as one with Christ. You are forever now part of the family of God through Jesus. As a joint heir with Christ, you also receive everything Christ has obtained from the Father. This includes every blessing and being glorified with Him (Romans 8:17).

What does this all mean when it comes to love? Most people often go hungry, starving and searching for love, thinking they are not cared about or loved by anyone special in a real quality or fulfilling way. They never fully understand or benefit from just how much they are loved and considered as special by God. John (3:16) says that God so loved the world that He gave His only begotten Son that whoever believes in Him should not perish but have ever-lasting life. What this means is that we were loved and cared for by God even before we became His children through the sacrifice of His Son Jesus.

Now that we are one and joint heirs with Christ, God loves us as He loves His Son Jesus (John 17:23). Yes, you heard me right. God loves us with the same love, concern, and adoration that He loves His only begotten Son, Jesus. This brings me to the picture of Jesus in the scriptures, where God looks down on Jesus being baptized and says, "This is my beloved Son in whom I am well pleased" (Matthew 3:17). What came to my spirit one day is that this is exactly the kind of fondness and love we as believers and children of God who are joined with Christ, and have been given His righteousness, receive directly from God. God adores and loves us. He looks upon you and me with the same eyes and heart of love and adoration He has for Jesus. God now sees us as clothed in Jesus' righteousness, due to the sacrifice and shedding of His body and blood. He sees us as joined with Christ, with the righteousness of Christ in us. We are truly loved with perfect love by God.

Today's Powerful Thought
My heart is not broken anymore! I am a beloved, cherished, adored, and cared for child of God.

Prayer
Father, when I am feeling frustration, despair, anxiety, and unloved, please remind me of my new identity in Christ Jesus and of how much You love, care about, and adore me. Please relieve my pain, agony, and loneliness. Help me to heal from a broken heart and to no longer settle and compromise in love. When I feel like it is impossible to survive and I feel unworthy, guilty, and ashamed, fill me with hope that love will come to me one day. In the name of Jesus, I pray. Amen.

DAY 2

NO VALUE

The truth is, if you don't see yourself as anything special, you tend to settle for less. This is all based on your past relationships. If you don't think you are anything special or fail to recognize your worth and value, you will not respect yourself. In your heart of hearts you may question, "Who could ever really respect and value me?" You may not feel confident that a special person who you love would ever choose to love you or even want to be your husband. Essentially, the quality of the love you have received in your most significant relationships forms the basis of your beliefs about your personal value and impacts your ability to love yourself and expect love from others. If you didn't receive quality love, such as from your parents, then you will feel less worthy of love. You will also be hungry for love at the same time. You will develop a desperate need to feel loved, valued, wanted, accepted, and acknowledged as important and special.

Recognize that the dissatisfaction and anxiety you experience as a result of not feeling genuinely loved and worthy of love contribute to you essentially compromising and approximating the feeling of genuine love. However, compromising only limits and blocks the potential to experience true love. The compromise of settling for less than true love, where there is no genuine mutual love and valuing and respecting of each other, will ultimately lead to other compromises. Consequently, you will inevitably feel worse and more miserable. You will also discover that you have limited your development and growth, which impacts all other areas of your life.

It is hard to recognize the detrimental effects of settling for less than you deserve, especially when you feel desperate to be loved. Your hunger for love may be constantly frustrated and never satisfied, making your quality of life worse. However, it is hard to consider the harmful consequences of settling for less than genuine, healthy love in the presence of experiencing the pain of loneliness and feeling unloved and uncared for.

Since you were only previously offered deficient love from other people, you never realized you actually deserved more. You may not be able to recognize how this sabotaged your sense of worth and value. If your sense of self was compromised in this way, then you will only see yourself as deficient and not capable of receiving love. Although you may desire love, you may not necessarily believe it is truly possible or likely for you.

Despite your best attempts to win and attract love from others, you may simply give in to the belief that you can only have relationships with people who love on a limited level or who don't really love you deeply. You may also discover that you tend to love people or form relationships with people where the quality of the love you experience resembles the deficient love you received from your parents and other significant people who compromised your sense of value, self-respect, and worthiness.

This ultimately makes you feel deficient as a person and, basically, like a disappointment, failure, and not good enough to deserve quality love from a good person.

With each compromise you make, you will also suffer from a diminished sense of feeling strong, capable, and competent. Limited love and shadows of love with people who claim to love you will only, in the end, reduce you and your life to a diminished and disarmingly crippled state of functioning on a level less than you are capable of. You will also have an unstable sense of self and purpose. The compromises you make to win love will result in the sacrifice of yourself and your personal happiness and fulfillment. To make life more tolerable, you may settle for being with people who will limit your capacity to mature, grow, and navigate challenges and opportunities to move forward and progress personally, professionally, and spiritually. It may limit your sense of purposeful destiny and meaning.

On the surface, settling may seem essential for survival and completely necessary if you are ever to have any sense of security, stability, connection, and fulfillment, or some form of happiness and love, no matter what form it comes in. Recognize that by compromising, you have likely given up more than you ever gained or realized could possibly be lost. To you, love has always been deficient and not what you hoped or dreamed about, so to settle seems like the inevitable, better choice. However, in the end, it will be detrimental.

What is the key to breaking this cycle? The real answer lies in your perception of how you see yourself and your beliefs. Recognize that you live by the level of your expectations and beliefs. Therefore, if you don't expect and believe that you are loved and that you can receive love, then you will function on the level of someone who thinks she is not good enough and, therefore, has to win love or compromise and settle for less. The truth, however, is that you cannot look to another human being to receive quality love on the level which heals your spirit and your broken, betrayed, wounded, and hurting heart, or makes you feel good enough, fulfilled, and loveable. However, you can be certain that God provides the answer that will never disappoint. When you realize just how much God values and loves you, it will help you to experience feeling truly deeply loved, cherished, cared for, and wanted. God, by sacrificing His own Son Jesus, and Jesus by allowing Himself to be sacrificed, both demonstrated complete, perfect love for you.

Do you see just how much you are richly loved, cared about, and favored? I call this selfless love, meaning, Jesus got nothing in return. He gave Himself up as a sacrificial offering from God without any gain to self—just to save you. God gave His own self through His begotten Son because He so loved us. Wonderful God gave up His own Son to save you.

You may ask yourself, "Why would God and Jesus do this if they gained nothing?" Recognize what God, your Abba Father, values. In essence, this demonstrated that God values and loves you and I. This is what He hoped to gain—a spiritual connection and fatherly relationship with you, through Jesus as the link. His heart hoped and longed to be in a relationship with you as your loving Father. Recognize just how much you are valued and loved. God Himself wanted to offer you love and receive your love. He values your love.

When I was given this revelation by God, I was personally dumbfounded. I could accept and acknowledge, as John (3:16) says, that God so loved us He gave His only begotten Son for us that we might be saved. However, when I received in my spirit that God sought our love and valued it as special and precious, I cried. My emotions overwhelmed me, as I felt the depth of God's love for us. I had never thought of my love as so very special, that God Himself holds it most dear. He holds me most dear in His heart. I am special to God, valued and loved by Him, and He is happy to receive my love and considers it special.

God loves you so much that He offered Jesus, the perfect Lamb of God, as the sacrifice for your sins. Do you receive what I am saying? Through His love and offering of His Son to be sacrificed, you received no more condemnation for your sins (Romans 8:1). This means you will never be punished for your sins, judged, or condemned. This is a finished work, meaning you are separated from your sins. The beautiful Savior, Jesus, took all of your sins into Himself and took the just punishment you deserved. Now this is truly love! You were given love, grace, mercy, and forgiveness. Jesus took your punishment and death sentence, which you deserved.

Just in case you don't still feel how much God loves you, here is something else you may consider. Through Jesus being offered as a sacrifice for your sins and through His finished work on the cross at Calvary, what you also received was the gift of Jesus' righteousness. Yes, this is what it means in 2 Corinthians 5:21, when it says Jesus became sin so that you would become the righteousness of God in Him (Jesus). An exchange took place on the cross during the sacrifice of Jesus. He took all of your sins (past, present, and future sins) and, in exchange, gave you the gift of His righteousness. You are covered and clothed in His righteousness.

The righteousness you receive when you accept Jesus cannot be undone or lost through some sin or negative performance on your part, since it is Jesus' righteousness. It is connected to Him and only based on how good and righteous Jesus is. It is not based on your goodness or level of sustained effort or performance. You have righteousness by grace. What does this mean? You are always and forever declared and recognized by God as righteous. This means you never have to fear being punished and condemned. Jesus fulfilled the law and bore your penalties for sin. His sacrifice for your sins was accepted and approved by God and so, you are now no longer subject to sin and death. Consider how much God loves you. This is God's mercy and grace.

Today's Powerful Thought
What a comfort it is to know just how much my Abba Father, God, loves me. I am unconditionally loved forever.

Prayer
Thank You, Abba Father, for offering Your perfect Son Jesus, who was sacrificed for my sins because You so loved me. Please help me to know just how much You love me. I come to You now to receive the perfect love You offer me unconditionally. Father thank You for loving me just as I am already. Thank You I never have to try to win Your love or do anything to keep it.

I accept Your love and warmth dear Father. Please let Your love deeply touch my heart now. Help my lonely heart to give in and lean on You, Father, I permit Your love to fill me with joy and peace, knowing You are always with me and care so deeply for me. I thank You Father for this opportunity to sit in this moment and bask in Your perfect love right now, focusing only on You and Jesus. I appreciate that I can do this without anxiety or fear of judgment and punishment because of Jesus and His sacrifice for my sins. Thank You, Jesus, that because of Your love for me You allowed Yourself to be sacrificed for me. Thank You that You took all my sins into Your own body, which was punished on my behalf, and gave me Your righteousness. Thank You, Jesus, that I am righteous and holy through You, by grace. In the name of Jesus, I pray. Amen.

DAY 3

NEW IDENTITY —NEW NATURE

Once you have received Christ Jesus as your personal Lord and Savior, it is time to turn your thoughts and your life, from the life you knew before, and establish yourself in the new identity and nature you have received in Christ. God sacrificed His Son Jesus to save you from condemnation and death. As a result, when you believe, you will experience a spiritual transformation, a shift in your very nature.

Through Adam, the nature of man was changed. Adam altered man's nature and consciousness to that of a sin nature and sin consciousness through his act of sin. You received a sin nature and death reigned by the trespass of one man, Adam, when he was disobedient and ate from the tree of knowledge of good and evil (Roman 5:12–19). That is why you were a sinner before you received grace and the gift of righteousness through Christ (Romans 5:17–21). That is why you lived the way you did before you believed. Therefore, just as by Adam's disobedience many were made sinners, by the obedience of Christ, many receive righteousness (Romans 5:19).

When Christ Jesus became your substitute on the cross, took your sins into Himself, and was punished in your place, you received His (Jesus') righteous nature once you believed by faith (Romans 5:17-19). In this exchange, by grace, you were given the free gifts of righteousness, justification, and life, whereby you are no longer a sinner, condemned, and subject to death. Yes, there was a wonderful exchange. Jesus took away your sins, and therefore your sin nature, and gave you His righteous nature. Therefore, your nature was altered forever when He gave you His righteousness in exchange for your sins. You have become the righteousness of God, in Christ Jesus (2 Corinthians 5:21).

Through the obedience of Christ, you no longer have a nature and spirit of sin (Romans 5:19). Christ transformed you. Now you have the nature of Christ. You are one with Christ and have His nature (Galatians 3:27-28, 1 Corinthians 6:17, John 1:12, 1 John 4:17). You are now identified with Christ. It is through Christ that you now have received your true nature and identity. Therefore, the grace of God reigned through righteousness leading to eternal life for believers, by Jesus Christ our Lord and Savior (Romans 5:21).

In your new identity and nature of righteousness in Christ, you are also now considered a child of God, an heir of God, and a joint-heir with Christ as well (Romans 8:16, John 1:12, 1 John 3:1-2, Romans 8:17). Yes, as stated in 1 John (3:1), do you see what great love the Father has lavished on you? God loves you so much that He made you His own child. He did this by permitting you to receive the very nature and righteous identity of Christ Jesus, whereby you have become one with His own Son, Jesus, and are now also a joint heir with Christ Jesus forever (Romans 8:16-19, Ephesians 3:6). As a child of God and a joint heir with

Christ Jesus, you are promised that you will also share in His (Jesus') glory (Romans 8:17). What this means is that you are now entitled to the same full rights, privileges, rewards, inheritance, and promises of God that Jesus is entitled to. God, your Father, has indeed lavished great love upon you!

Further, when God looks at you, He sees you as one and the same as Jesus. This is because you have received His nature of righteousness and no longer have your old sin nature. You have received this free gift by grace and mercy. Therefore, you need not suffer the fear of judgment, condemnation, punishment, and rejection You no longer have to see yourself as defined by your past, the history of your family's sins, your sins, shame, guilt, the compromises and mistakes you made, and what others did to you. You have been reborn in the nature of Christ Jesus.

Recognize the divinity you are connected to. While you may still struggle to recognize who you really are, I encourage you to forget history, past failures, bad relationships, and how others defined and valued you. God's grace and the gifts you have received in Christ are much more powerful than what Adam did, your sins, and the past (Romans 5:15). Therefore, your life today can overflow with God's grace and blessings.

Confess this truth every time you consider yourself or begin to evaluate your performance and the way others perceive and treat you. I urge you to reflect on the truth, established on the firm foundation of the Word of God. Take time to read scriptures, like the ones quoted in this book, which introduce you to your real identity in Jesus. You have received a new life of freedom, a new nature in Jesus, and the right to experience every good thing in your life. Your sins and past don't define how successful you will be or how much love and fulfillment you will experience in your life. You don't have to feel limited and condemned. Yes, a full life of love and healthy relationships are part of God's intended blessings for you. You will not receive this based on you or your efforts, but rather because of the finished work of Jesus on the cross and the righteousness of Christ Jesus, which you have received. Therefore, turn your thoughts away from your old beliefs about who you are and the life you lived before. Instead, focus your thoughts on the life, nature, and identity you have in Christ Jesus and on God's amazing love for you. You are a loved child of God!

The analogy of the marriage bond may further help you understand how you are now connected to Jesus and transformed in your spirit by His righteousness. This special bond between you and Christ is what is alluded to when Christ is sometimes called the bridegroom and husband, and the church is inferred to be the bride or wife of Christ (Mark 2:19, 2 Corinthians 11:2, Ephesians 5:27-32). You may ask, "Just who is the church?" You are. Therefore, you are now considered the bride of Christ. When a man and a woman are married, the husband and wife become one, unseparated, one and the same. They are meant to be connected in nature. They become one flesh (Ephesians 5:31-32). Therefore, a man, for example, is encouraged to love and consider his wife in the same way he would his own body, as they are one and the same flesh. This marriage analogy is meant to symbolize our beautiful relationship of being one with Jesus, our merciful Savior and bridegroom. In your bond of relationship with Christ, you have received His Spirit of righteousness and have a new identity in Him. In your union with Christ, your transformation is not simply symbolic. In reality, the very nature of who you are is now transformed into the righteous nature of Christ. Your bond with Christ can never be broken. It is permanent and unbreakable. Therefore, there is nothing you can do to compromise your new nature of righteousness, because it is received from Christ and based on the quality of His righteousness, goodness, and obedience, and not your own.

When Jesus Christ died for you, He satisfied the law and fulfilled it when He paid your penalty for sins on the cross at the Crucifixion. Thus, through His death for your sins, He fulfilled the law and broke the bondage of sin, death, and the law in your life. Further, because Christ took your place and you are considered to have died and risen with Christ, receiving His righteousness by grace, you have been released from the law, which once bound you, and are now one with Christ (Romans 6:3–14, Romans 7:4–6).

Sin is no longer your master and you are no longer under the law but under grace (Romans 6:14). Also, since Jesus died on your behalf and the law has been fulfilled through Him, you are free from your marriage bond to the law. However, you, I, and every believer need not long for a new husband. We have a new marriage union with Christ. Having died through the body of Christ, your marriage to the law is over, and you are free from the law which once bound you (Romans 7:4). You are now one with Christ, who raised you from the dead. Through this marriage you receive the gift of His righteousness, His identity, and His Spirit (Romans 8:9). You now belong to and are one with Christ (Romans 7:4). You are released from the law so that you now walk in the new way of the Spirit and not in the old way of sin and the old way of the written code, which condemned the sin in you to death (Romans 7:6–11). Now you are righteous through Christ.

Therefore, in Christ, you have become a new creature, and old things and your old self of a sin nature have passed away (2 Corinthians 5:17, Romans 7:6–11). You no longer walk in the flesh but in the Spirit, are of God, and have been reconciled to Him through Jesus Christ (2 Corinthians 5:18). God made Christ to be sin for us so that through Him you might be made the righteousness of God in Christ (2 Corinthians 5:21).

You have received God's righteousness through Christ and are declared forever righteous based on Christ Jesus' good standing and righteousness. You are one with Christ Jesus. Further, you are identified with Christ. You have His identity. You are a beloved child of God. God adores and loves you the same way He loves and adores Jesus (John 17:23). Indeed, that makes you more than worthy and good enough. It also frees you from the bondage of shame, guilt, condemnation, and your past. You are beautiful in Christ!

Today's Powerful Thought
When I struggle with my self-worth, I can stop and recall that I have received the righteous nature of God through Christ Jesus and am a loved child of God.

Prayer
Dear Abba Father, as I reflect on the price Christ Jesus paid for me, I am feeling blessed and loved. I acknowledge and graciously accept His righteousness, which He gave me. I thank You Father that I am now

one with Christ Jesus and have His identity and am part of Your family, Father. Thank You that I am reconciled with You, Father. I feel so loved knowing that because of Christ Jesus, I am completely transformed in His image, and am no longer bound by my sin, brokenness, and history. I no longer have to feel ashamed, guilty, not good enough, less than worthy, and unlovable. I know I deserve every good thing because I am Your child and because of the righteous nature of Christ Jesus, which I have received. I no longer must suffer from history, past trauma, or the things I have done and what others did to me. I am no longer defined or limited by these things. Help me to recall this constantly. When I look at myself in the mirror, please help me to see myself the way You see me. Help me to see the Spirit of Christ Jesus in me. Dear Father, help me to no longer live backwards, stuck in the life and traumas of my past. Help me to move confidently forward in the Spirit of my new life in Christ Jesus. Help me to have a confident expectation of good, because I am one with Christ Jesus and Your beloved, righteous child. In Jesus I live and pray. Amen.

DAY 4

LOOKING FOR LOVE — SEARCHING FOR SOMEONE TO LOVE ME

While God has given you a new Spirit of righteousness through Christ, and you have become a new creature in Christ (2 Corinthians 5:17), it does not mean that now the needs of the flesh are forever absent and that you won't still desire to be loved or want a mate. It is natural to love and desire a mate. God told Eve her desire would be for her husband, to please him (Genesis 3:16). Eve was created to be Adam's helper and partner (Genesis 2:18). She was made from his body. The two were of one flesh and were bonded together spiritually (Genesis 2:21–24). She was called Adam's woman to signify that she was taken (made) out of man (Genesis 2:23). This reflects their partnership and spiritual bond. Would it, therefore, be so absurd to believe that you too would deeply desire a mate? Don't forget that God Himself gave you this desire. He declared that it was not good for man to be alone, without a partner (Genesis 2:18). Therefore, I encourage you to not be so intimidated by or afraid of the gift of love in a relationship with a partner and mate. A good relationship with a mate is a blessing to your life, which benefits both of you.

In societies around the world, women are increasingly encouraged to actively seek the right person. You are advised to look for certain characteristics in a man and date until you discover the perfect partner for you. There are many articles and books on how to do all of this correctly, and many offer you solutions on how to attract and be desired by an eligible mate. You are offered tips on how to attract the right person by making yourself more beautiful, appealing, accommodating, and irresistible, thus guaranteeing you will make him fall in love with you. You are encouraged to focus on how to please a man, satisfy him, and meet his needs, while maintaining his interest and faithfulness. You are told competition is stiff and other women are basically your enemy. Your need for a mate is only amplified further by every ad and commercial, as well as music and the general scenery around you, which depict either happy couples or loneliness and isolation.

Unfortunately, each experience in the world makes your own need and lack all the more intensely felt. All things considered, it is difficult not to experience a desperate longing to feel loved, accompanied by anxiety and absolute dread of a life of being alone forever, unloved. You may likely suffer angst and uncertainty about ever having the fantasy love relationship you desire with a mate. Everything in life seems to set the mood for you to anxiously chase after love. In fact, you may experience the almost instinctively driven urge to actively pursue and hunt for your own happiness in a relationship with the right man.

While it is likely that you have been afraid of the gift of real love eluding you, have you ever considered that real love is chasing after you? However, who could be the one chasing after you? Who loves you so faithfully and passionately that he is willing to run after you and patiently endure all things with you? Who values you, offers you support, empathy, kindness, and understanding? Who offers to help you? Who offers you relief and willingly bares your burdens for you? Who listens with a listening heart? Who, despite your difficulties and struggles, calls out to you, does not close the door, and seeks to be near you? Who completely, sees you, accepts you as you are and woos you anyway? Who bids you come receive love? Who sings you a constant love song?

The answer is revealed in the book of the Bible, Song of Solomon. Jesus is the one who loves you with genuine, compassionate, everlasting love. Within the poetry of the Songs you see a picture of Jesus wooing the woman. He is inviting her to not be scared, but to receive His love without fear. In Song of Solomon (3:6), the groom comes perfumed with myrrh and frankincense, depicting how Jesus came to be sacrificed for you and to bring you into a new life, resurrected and alive with Him. You are now invited into the new household, the house of God, and are received and welcomed as a child of God. You are now part of God's family. Do you see how the groom (Jesus) adores the bride (you), who is adorned with His righteousness now that you have become one with Him?

Reading the Song of Solomon is a wonderful way to invite the experience of the intensity and earnestness of the genuine, never wavering, eternal love of God and the love of Jesus for you. The

Song of Solomon reveals that you can accept Jesus' and God's love without fear. It reveals that God desperately loves you and longs to give you a better life. He wants to make you a part of His family and give you a home. The groom (Jesus) calls to you with His love song so you may experience the gift of real love, freedom from sin and death, and a better life. He calls you to be one with Him and to receive the gift of the righteousness of God in Him.

You are called to now become one with Jesus, to receive His Spirit, and to be bound to Him. You are a new creation in Christ, and have the nature and identity of Jesus—similarly to how Eve was formed out of Adam—and are one with Him (2 Corinthians 5:17-21, Romans 8:9). We are reminded in Ephesians (3:18-19) that it is difficult for us to fully comprehend the true breadth, length, height, and depth of the love of Christ and the fullness of God's love, which surpasses all of our knowledge and understanding. God truly does love you.

You need not compromise yourself or values to receive love any longer. Your hunt for perfect love is over! Be reminded today that you are loved already. I encourage you to come into the presence of God and Jesus to receive their love. They have been chasing after you passionately. They value your love and yearn to receive it. It is a treasured gift to them. You are special to God and Jesus. This is why God sent His Son to die for you, and time and time again lovingly pursues you—not to punish or condemn you, but to simply offer you love.

With His love He gives life, peace, and joy. His love for you is so powerful, sincere, and selfless that He gave up His own Son Jesus as a sacrifice for you—to save you from punishment and death. Jesus invites you to stop chasing love and simply receive earnest, genuine, and beautiful love from God and Himself. This is a love that will never disappoint. His love makes you whole, so that you will no longer seek fulfillment, worthiness, and a sense of value from your relationship with a mate. No human relationship can give you this. Only God's love can satisfy what you truly need and have been desiring in a relationship with someone else.

When you receive love in your relationship with God and Christ Jesus, then you will finally feel loved and good enough to be loved by another. You will experience a sense of value, worth, and fulfillment, which makes you feel complete and whole. It is only then that you will truly be capable of loving on the deepest and fullest level possible. It is then that you will enjoy a full and healthy relationship with a partner for the rest of your life.

People generally learn to love on the level that they have experienced love from other people in their lives. However, when you truly experience the love of God in a deeper relationship with Him, you will learn to love another on the level you receive love from God. Likewise, you will simply offer love and receive love from another without compromising yourself, playing games, and following ill-advised worldly wisdom on how to win love, which does not yield the fruit of the love you desire. Only one who has become one with Christ and experiences the love of God can truly feel perfectly loved and then love in the way a husband and wife are asked to love one another.

Today's Powerful Thought
The hunt is over. I am valued and
loved fully by God and Jesus.

Prayer
Oh, dear sweet Father, forgive me for the times I forget to turn back around and come to You, who always desires and longs to offer me the opportunity to receive Your perfect and complete love. Thank You for always enduring everything with me, no matter the misfortunes, struggles, and trials of life. Thank You that You long to bring me joy and a full life. I earnestly want to receive Your quality love and ask You to help me draw closer to You and feel Your compassionate, perfect love for me. Help me to not be afraid of Your love, but to instead enjoy the experience of what it feels like, as You, Father, draw closer to me in love. My loving Father, thank You for Jesus, who connects with me in love. Thank You for patiently enduring and welcoming me in love. Thank You, Father, for valuing my love as something You accept, value, and cherish in Your own heart. I open my own heart to receive Your beautiful love right now. In the name of Jesus, I pray. Amen.

DAY 5

THE GIFT OF LOVE

The beautiful gift of love is a treasure bestowed by God. You have this beautiful gift right now, available to you in your personal relationship with God and Jesus. When it comes to love with a mate or partner, likewise, it too is a precious gift that God bestows. A partner will love you, as Christ loves the church. You will elevate and help each other mature in love, as well as in your overall spiritual maturity. Just consider for a moment how very special this kind of love is. In 1 Corinthians (13:1), the beauty of love is described. It says that of all the gifts you may ever receive, love is by far the greatest one. This suggests that we as individuals feel empty, and life itself feels empty, meaningless, and contrived without love.

But what is love really? What are its characteristics? How do you recognize it? What does it look and feel like? How is it demonstrated, communicated, and imparted by a partner in a real relationship? How do you know what God intended when He asked you to love one another as Christ so loved us? In looking to 1 Corinthians (13) once more, for wisdom in love, you are given guidance by the author, who himself had a divine love experience of the most profound kind.

The apostle Paul, who wrote 1 Corinthians, personally had an encounter with Jesus on the road to Damascus. Paul, who condemned and persecuted Christians and hated Jesus, had a life-altering encounter with Jesus when he was on his way to arrest and persecute the followers of Jesus. Paul himself writes about this encounter of love and grace in his testimony (Acts 9:1–9, Acts 22:6–16, Acts 26:9–20). It was such a beautiful encounter of love and grace that it transformed Paul, a man who had devoted his entire life to upholding the law and saw Jesus as his enemy. It altered and transformed Paul, who would come to personify love, compassion, mercy, and grace, and would teach these things to all the world.

In the presence of Jesus, Paul experienced the gift of love and grace. Paul was not condemned or punished. He was offered mercy and grace, which flowed from nothing less than perfect love. He experienced the merciful, compassionate, understanding, forgiving, and gentle love of Christ Jesus.

In Timothy (1:12–16), Paul writes about his experience of receiving Jesus' love, grace, and mercy because he had acted ignorantly in unbelief. He wrote, "The grace of our Lord overflowed for me with the faith and love that are in Christ Jesus." (Timothy 1:14) The original King James Version (KJV) translates this to say, "And the grace of our Lord was **exceeding abundant** with faith and love which are in Christ Jesus." (1 Timothy 1:14) Realize the immeasurable level of overabundant, prolific, never-ending grace and love that Paul attempted to describe. Jesus' love and grace affected him so deeply that it transformed him and changed his life forever. Paul experienced genuine love and grace, which in turn separated him from his history, sin, and condemnation, and impacted his identity, sense of self, and his relationships with others. His letters to friends and believers demonstrate how Paul in turn offered compassion, love, and grace to others. Paul had a clear understanding of the nature of true love and the grace which flows from love. This is why he wrote about love being the greatest of all the gifts (1 Corinthians 13).

Love is an experience. However, what is the experience of love really like? What are the qualities and characteristics of love? Paul (in 1 Corinthians 13:4) adds clarity and describes the experience of love more clearly. Love is defined as being patient and kind. It is not envious. This means it is not jealous and withholding or invested only in one's own needs and ambitions. It is not boastful, arrogant, or rude. It does not insist on its own way. We see in this that love is compassionate and not selfishly motivated. Nor is it irritable, angry, or resentful. This means that in love, you don't wound and punish or try to win at all costs, feeling justified because you feel wronged. It also means love is not revengeful, mean, and spiteful. It is considerate of the other and values the other above all. Love does not rejoice in wrongdoing, but instead it tells the truth and rejoices in the truth. There are no lies and deception in love. Love demonstrates the capacity to bear all things. It is hopeful and believes. Love endures all things. Love is permanent, and is not fickle or subject to alteration, meaning it does not come to an end or ceases. Love exists and flows forever. Love reassures you that you can depend on its constancy, forgiveness, and faithfulness, without condemnation.

If you explore the nature of love more deeply, you will realize other key qualities that are inferred by Paul's experience of genuine love, which are also applicable to a relationship with a mate. These include growing more deeply in genuine, mutual empathy, commitment, acceptance, understanding, grace, forgiveness, and faithfulness. As a couple, it means you change, learn, and grow together, allowing each other space to mature, while having patience with each other. It suggests you persevere as you go through life's problems and journey over time together. Your love endures misfortunes and suffering, but sustains, despite how painful life gets. It does not yield, but is solid and dependable despite life's many pressures and burdens.

Love on the level that Paul writes about suggests that you bear all things, including disappointments, problems, and life transitions that you both go through over time, over the course of your lives. Despite how difficult and painful things become, your love does not transfer to another. It never ends. It endures and remains consistent. In fact, as you each grow and mature, especially on a spiritual level in your personal relationship with God and Jesus, you grow even more deeply in compassionate love with your mate.

The love that Paul experienced was so profound that it healed his broken spirit and wounded, angry, condemning heart. Paul's profound experience demonstrates the power of the love of God and Jesus. You too will be transformed when you open your heart to receive God and Jesus' love. Only their love fully satisfies. Their love will heal and make you whole. You will experience feeling worthy, good enough, valued, wanted, genuinely cared about, and deeply considered. When you experience the love of God and Christ, like Paul, your spirit, heart, mind, sense of self, identity, value, worth, meaning, and purpose will be transformed. You will also experience the amazing, life-altering, loving grace of God, as Paul did. Jesus' love and the love of God will do the same for you as it did for Paul.

As love applies to your own love relationship with a partner, Jesus encourages you to love one another in the way He demonstrated love to Paul. These are the true qualities of love. Likewise, God wants you to do it His way, as Jesus demonstrated, so that you can grow your relationship based on the foundation of the principles He set. This is the only way that love will really last. Further, perhaps the most important part of learning to love as Christ and of growing more deeply in love and having a lasting, loving relationship with another, is to make your spiritual relationship with God and Jesus your priority. As you spend time with both and deepen your personal spiritual relationship with both, you will experience love even more deeply. The love you experience as a beloved child of God will become the foundation of your love with a partner.

Today's Powerful Thought
Right now, I have received the beautiful gift of the gracious, forgiving, life-altering, healing, and transformative love of Abba Father and Jesus.

Prayer
Abba Father, thank You for the love I receive from both You and Jesus, and the benefits of Your love for me. I acknowledge that without Your love, I would suffer from such deep emptiness. Your love heals and

transforms me into a better person, when I receive Your patient, kind, gracious, forgiving, respectful, gentle, unselfish, generous, peaceful, tender, hopeful, genuine, truthful, faithful, never-ending, and enduring love. When I receive Your love, I know You welcome me to experience feeling worthy, and deeply loved, valued, and cared for. Please help me to experience these feelings more deeply right now. Help me to love myself and others with the same love with which You love me. Help me to love in a way that reflects the nature and quality of Your love. As I experience Your love, help me to give love more freely, and to love more fully and completely, with kindness, compassion, empathy, understanding, forgiveness, and patience. Help me to love with a big, open heart and to embrace each person I meet with Your beautiful love. Help me to, like Paul, bask in the gift of Jesus' beautiful love and to allow it to transform me. Help me to love You and others more dearly each moment of the day, Abba. In Jesus I pray. Amen.

DAY 6

PATIENCE IN LOVE—WAITING FOR GOD'S BEST

So, if you are like most people, you may sometimes struggle with being patient. The act of being patient can feel restrictive and anxiety provoking. Exercising patience while waiting for love is no less difficult or painful, when you are waiting for that relationship with someone special to unfold in your life. I am speaking about a mate who intentionally walks with God. I refer to that special someone who will genuinely love you as Christ loves us. This is a man who does not follow after his fleshly desires and needs, but loves without compromising himself or devaluing you.

It is easy to grow impatient, wondering when it will finally happen for you. Perhaps your heart has been disappointed in the past. Perhaps you fear that this may never happen or that you missed out on your best and last opportunity for love. Perhaps you feel you are growing too old and life is passing you by. Every year may signal yet another year spent alone, and you may wonder and ask, "When will you remember me, Lord? Will it ever happen?" You may fear it never will.

What if you shifted from a fearful and disillusioned position to one where you draw closer to God in these moments? What if you chose to live a life free of striving and trying so hard and instead decided to rest? What would happen if you stopped striving and trying so hard? What do I mean? Sometimes, we try to help God along by pushing forward to find the right person and right opportunity for love to unfold. You may find yourself forcing things or making decisions without God or against His will. Look back at all those wasted efforts in compromising and trying to make someone love you or pushing for a relationship to develop and grow. Think of the times you compromised and settled for less than the love you wanted or perhaps the times you convinced your heart that it was really love, only to find out later that it was a lie. Think of the time and energy you wasted, as well as the resources and the things you lost along the way. Consider how you suffered emotionally and were wounded.

Wisdom comes from God, and you can trust it will always be for your good. God offers you the opportunity to rest in His efforts. This means you can cease striving and trying to make love happen while benefitting from allowing God to take the lead. In the waiting period, you can trust God. His Word assures you that there is no fear in love (1 John 4:18). He loves you and wants the best for you.

You can rest being certain that His grace will abound toward you. God is able to make all grace abound toward you, so that you will always have sufficiency in all things (2 Corinthians 9:8). The New Revised Standard Version (NRSV) translates this as, "God is able to provide you with every blessing in abundance." Not only does

God offer grace by the sacrifice of His Son but He also offers grace for you to receive blessings in every area of your life. This includes the blessing of a partner, a man who God Himself provides by His grace. If you believe this truth in your spirit, then you can let go of all of your fears, worries, anxiety, ceaseless striving, and efforts to make it all happen by yourself. God promises His grace will abound toward you and deliver to you many blessings. Grace provides.

It does not require you to orchestrate the entire thing. While you may have to engage in personal and spiritual preparation, follow God's will, let Him prepare the way, permit Him to lead your actions, and let Him open and close doors, so that He will place you in the right place at the right time, with the people He chooses. By grace, the effort on your part will be extraordinarily less than you may imagine.

Listen to me clearly. Be at rest and let God do the heavy lifting. He takes pleasure in providing for His children (you). Consider how valued and loved you are. He sacrificed His Son to save you. What else would He not do for you? God cares for you so much that He wants you to be blessed as your heart desires. Perhaps He is the very one who put that desire in your heart for a mate in the first place. Examine God's intentions toward you. He always operates in grace towards you. This takes the form of Him generously giving and you receiving His best. When God knew you needed a sacrifice, to save you He offered the best sacrifice, Jesus, His own Son. Likewise, in choosing a husband for you, He will offer His best choice available for you.

What am I saying? God loves you, cares about you, and deeply considers what is His best for you. In this waiting period for a mate, consider that if you rush in or compromise, settle, or even try to force God's hand, and rush the process along, you will be compromising on receiving God's very best choice. Of all the valuable gifts you could receive, recognize what God is offering you. It is worth more than all the money, gold, diamonds, worldly titles, prestige, and worldly acknowledgment in the world. What you have the hope of receiving is quality love, which is exceptionally rare and precious, in a relationship with someone where you can both aspire to love on the level Christ loves the church.

God asks you to trust Him and let Him guide you. He wants to help you grow, change, and love more deeply. He offers you love and asks you to lean on His grace. He asks you to feel reassured that by grace you will receive His best for you. He asks you to experience His love and kindness for a sense of worth, value, and feeling good enough to be loved. He asks you to seek a relationship with Him first and to let Him love you perfectly.

In this time of waiting, draw closer to God. He wants to heal your hurts, and make you whole and one with Christ. He welcomes you into His family and household. God is offering you His heart and His perfect, unconditional love. He is also offering you the love of Jesus. This is so you can experience real love and no longer compromise or be controlled and manipulated by sin, lack, need, and desire. He wants to prepare you and your future husband to be able to love each other as God desires. Be patient and trust God. Ask Him to help you be patient, love, discern love, and to strengthen you to rest in Him and to trust with complete faith. Also, rest by allowing Him to prepare you for this next stage and role in life. Focus on your relationship with God and Jesus and on receiving their abundant, perfect love. Let them provide you with their complete and perfect love.

You may wonder, "How will I ever be able to be patient and wait?" Be reminded of the promise to Paul in 2 Corinthians 12:9: "My grace is sufficient for thee; for my strength is made perfect in weakness." You are offered Jesus' assurance that if you will come to Him and draw from His strength and love, in your moments of weakness and feeling tested beyond what you can bare, He (Jesus) will offer you rest and peace. Then He will take on the challenge Himself on your behalf. By grace, you will get through this. This means He will provide whatever is lacking and accomplish whatever is necessary when you rely on Him in faith. God's grace will abound and provide you with every blessing.

Today's Powerful Thought
I can stop my worry and striving for I know that
by grace I will receive the gift of love, also knowing
I am already loved perfectly by God and Jesus.

Prayer
Jesus, thank You that You love me so much, You died
on the cross for me so that by grace I may receive
no condemnation and everlasting life, as a child of
God. Thank You, Abba Father, that Your love and
grace abound toward me. Thank You for desiring
to bless me with every blessing, including receiving
the special blessing of a husband. Thank You, Father,
that You care so much about me that You provide for
me so that I don't have to strive so tirelessly. Thank

You that You simply ask that I trust You will provide the best for me. Help me not to grow impatient and distressed, or to despair in my time of waiting. Thank You that You love me, and I receive Your gift of love right now in this moment. Thank You that I always receive Your love, no matter what. Please guide me, Father, and let Your will be done in my life. I submit to Your will. I give You full permission to operate in my life and help me to receive that very special person in my life, in Your perfect time, and in the way You desire of me and him. In Jesus I pray. Amen.

DAY 7
WAITING — PART TWO

A conflict within can often arise from two commonly occurring dilemmas. It may be hard to be patient when you don't trust God completely. The other problem may be that you don't really believe that someone special may be able to genuinely love you and treat you with genuine, loving intention.

Waiting to receive love is difficult. Often, prior to learning to wait, you may endure disappointment, loneliness, doubt, and struggles with needs and desires. Waiting may ask you to believe in what you don't see. Worldly wisdom says things don't just happen on their own. It says you have to make it happen. Desire and loneliness urge you to chase after love or to settle for what seems close enough. It tells you love is not the important thing—security and material things secure your happiness and fulfillment. When your impatience for love grows steadily more desperate, you may compromise. You may require your heart to betray or deceive you into thinking you are not compromising.

The key to waiting is to acknowledge and appreciate it as a time of preparation. It is also necessary to receive it as God's best for you at this present time. I've learned that you should only get married to someone you genuinely love, who genuinely loves you in return, where you are both getting your need to be loved and sense of self-worth from a personal relationship with God. To do otherwise is destructive and will kill many things in your life. You can focus on this basic truth in the waiting season.

The time of preparation is a gift. Therefore, during this time, focus more on developing a closer relationship with God and Jesus. Focus on the experience of feeling loved by them both. Pray earnestly during this time and ask God to receive the gift and blessing of a husband in His perfect time and according to His plan and purpose. Enrich your prayer by asking Him to receive a husband who purposefully walks with Him. Ask for a husband who loves Him and Jesus, and who acknowledges that he is saved by grace through the sacrifice of Jesus. Ask that he will love you as Christ asks him to love his bride. Further, ask God to prepare you in every way, including spiritually, to be a good wife. Ask for help with seeking His love, wisdom, and guidance. Focus on developing your gifts and engaging in your purposeful calling, to the glory of God, during your waiting period.

Consider all the ways you need to heal and grow as a person. The benefit is that this will ensure you don't continue in patterns and habits based on needs and desires, which will destroy your happiness and fulfillment in life, as well as your relationships with others. In this season of waiting, perhaps, God is actually waiting on you, not vice versa. He is waiting on you to engage in your own growth and to seek Him more fully. He wants you to turn your heart, life, thoughts, emotions, behaviors, needs, desires, relationships, plans for your future, and your overall destiny over to Him. He wants an intimate relationship with you. He wants to love you and provide protection, direction, and all you need. He wants you to come deeper into a relationship with Him so that He can heal you and satisfy your needs and desires.

During the time of waiting, also consider why you want a mate. Is it to satisfy areas of lack and need? Is it so you don't feel unworthy, unloved, not valued, invalidated, lonely, undesired, unwanted, insecure, and ashamed? Do you find it difficult to control your desires? Are there difficulties and painful experiences which may be triggering your urgency? Did someone else make you feel humiliated or wound your heart so deeply that you can't seem to recover? Just consider for a moment your real areas of deepest pain, need, and emptiness. Then consider this. Are you seeking a mate from a desire to heal areas of your deepest pain and hurt? Is it possible you may be unknowingly hoping that a longed-for husband or partner will do what only God and Jesus are able to?

You may be seeking love and healing from the wrong source. You will find that no human being can heal your wounded heart or your areas of deepest pain, need, unworthiness, and emptiness. No human being can accomplish what only your relationship with God and Jesus can do. I encourage you to consider drawing closer to God and Jesus for the love you are seeking. Only their perfect love—and no one else's—can give you what you need. Through grace and the sacrifice of Jesus, you received the righteousness of God (2 Corinthians 5:21). Your hope for love is fulfilled in Christ. The love you receive takes away your painful history and sins of the past. It takes away condemnation, humiliation, shame, guilt, and unworthiness. It heals your deepest pain and your broken heart (Romans 8:1, Isaiah 53:4–5). By the sacrifice of Jesus and the punishment He suffered on your behalf, you have been healed. Christ Jesus is the answer you have been seeking. You don't have to compromise yourself to receive Jesus or God's love.

I caution you that your healing comes from another source entirely—Christ. Also, recognize that God may not bestow the gift of that very special man in your life until your healing and growth takes place. You may have to be healed to be ready for your mate. In this season of waiting, you may also be required to be patient, as the mate God intends for you to marry is also being prepared and healed from his deepest pain, condemnation, unworthiness, and a broken heart, through Christ, so he can become a suitable husband for you. Yes, God wants the very best for you. He will not just let you compromise yourself or settle for less than the best He has to offer His very special child—you.

In the waiting season, His silence does not always mean no. It may mean not now. But in the waiting period, as you just read, there is much to be achieved with Him. However, it can only be accomplished when you make being in a relationship with Him and Christ your priority. Now be still and let it be accomplished through God according to His will and purpose for your life. Don't try to force the process or skip the waiting period. God loves you. The gift of His love heals. Remember, you are healed in Christ (Isaiah 53:5) and have the gift of grace in the beloved (Ephesians 1:6). In time, you will receive the promise.

Today's Powerful Thought

During the waiting period, I will let God's perfect love heal me and focus on how Christ took away all my sins, pain, and unworthiness on the cross.

Prayer

Abba Father, help me to be patient during my waiting season. Please help me to experience Your love, which heals. Help me to experience the gift of Your grace and no condemnation, which I received through Christ Jesus. Thank You for Your promise of a new and better life. Thank You that I am loved, and that Christ took all my sins, pain, and unworthiness into Himself. Thank You that I have received Your righteousness, through Christ. Please help me to remember that You have Your best in store for me, and I don't have to worry about being blessed or having a loving relationship with a mate. In Jesus I pray. Amen.

DAY 8

LESSONS IN EXERCISING PATIENCE

Witnessing that this period of waiting is positively a period of profound lessons, and personal and spiritual growth, you will still be required to actively exercise patience in a way that quiets your spirit, calms your anxiety, and reassures you. This requires a spiritual solution to be able to maintain strength and hope. Given the weight of the learning and maturity process you will experience, it is important to focus on the value of the growth and healing experience, and of exercising patience.

The first step is to courageously accept that it is better to be patient and wait until both you and your future husband are ready. What you must also accept is that your mate is also being prepared for his promotion to eventually becoming your husband. He too is experiencing a period of personal spiritual preparation, growth, and maturity. Like you, he is being healed of destructive and negative patterns of thinking, behaviors, and his own personal history of pain. Unquestionably, God is also healing his heart with His love and helping him to learn to love a mate as Christ loves the church (Ephesians 5:25).

I am not saying that both you and a mate will be perfect and totally without flaws, difficulties, desires, needs, anxieties, and lessons yet to learn once you do meet each other and begin your relationship. On the contrary, you will discover that you need to help each other continue to grow. However, there is benefit in waiting until God in His wisdom has appointed that the season of love is ready to bloom and grow between the two of you. Permit yourself the gift of patiently waiting to receive what is going to be better for you, because you are in a better place personally and your mate is also being prepared to be in a better place as well.

Find comfort in knowing that during this time, God is working behind the scenes to place everything in position. Just because you don't know His plans or see God working doesn't mean He is not working on your behalf and on behalf of your future husband. Receive in faith that God orchestrates everything according to His divine perfect will and timing. You can trust Him to do the best He can for you to help you on your life journey. Experience His peace and be comforted by knowing that He sacrificed His own Son Jesus for you. Therefore, this is proof enough that you can trust Him and that He loves and cares for you.

It is also important to recognize that even after you meet your potential mate, the exercise of waiting patiently is still beneficial. It will continue to be necessary for you to exercise patience and wait until love is ready. In this time of patience, refocus on your relationship with God and Jesus. Your relationship with God and Jesus will help you feel more encouraged, hopeful, loved, and cared for. This is especially true when you are challenged with feeling isolated or disillusioned. So what else can you do while you patiently wait until love is ready?

You will benefit in these moments from listening to worship music. Listen to spiritual music and worship God. While you will gain much from going to church and worshiping in that community environment, saturate your home environment with praise and worship music. Go deeper into praise. When you worship, rejoice, sing praises to God, and give glory to God, God will respond (Isaiah 42:10–14). Isaiah says that when you praise, the Lord will be stirred with zeal on your behalf and will go forth and triumph over your enemies. He will do the fighting for you. Therefore, lift your voice in praise, sing, and worship God without restraint. Lift your hands in praise and dance if you feel like it. Allow your spirit to be open—in fellowship with God—without restraint and glorify God with praises. Acknowledge how great He is and how much He has done.

Focus on His love for you and allow yourself to receive His rich love even more intimately. Permit His presence to overflow within your entire spirit and body. Pour your heart out to God and express everything you feel. Ask Him to help you feel loved, hopeful, encouraged, and cared for. Ask Him for patience.

As you continue to listen to music, allowing it to saturate all of your senses and experiences, shift your focus to welcoming the presence of God and Jesus. Permit yourself to embrace the warmth of their rich and satisfying loving presence. Ask them both to come nearer to you so you may feel their presence and love. Welcome them. There is no need for fear or anxiety. Remember, God loves you. He also wants to be closer to you and deepen your relationship with Him.

Don't fear receiving judgment or harm. Expect good and to feel completely loved and accepted for who you are, as you are. Remember, Christ was offered as a sacrifice in your place already, so fear not. Seek comfort in approaching the Father and your Savior Christ Jesus, who love you more deeply than any love you have received and can conceive of. You are so special that the gift of grace was offered through the sacrifice of Jesus to separate you from harm and death. What compassion the Father feels for you, which He demonstrated by His love offering of Jesus in your place! You are truly important to God.

God loves you like the father of the prodigal son, who poured out his heart as he welcomed his wayward son back home. His son had strayed and lived a sinful life, yet when exhausted and broken from his riotous living, his father warmly hugged him and treated him like a prince (Luke 15:11-32). There was no harshness or judgment, only love. As a believer in Jesus, you are a child of God, and to God a valued and loved member of His household and kingdom (John 1:12, Ephesians 2:19-22). You are very precious to Him.

Are you ready? Do you want to receive His offering of love toward you? Simply say, "Father, I am ready to receive your love. Please come sit close to me. Jesus please draw nearer. Let me receive and deeply feel Your love for me right now, right here, with You and God both next to me. Thank you, Father, for Your gift of perfect love." What I am really saying is—all you have to do is ask or give permission in your heart and it will be done. The exact words you use are not important. The Father already knows your intentions and what you desire.

Additionally, as you listen to worship music and engage in singing and praise, you will experience your spirit and emotions being lifted and positively charged. You will also feel God's perfect love for you. This is an opportunity to also experience the peace of Christ. In the experience of deeper intimacy with God and Jesus, you will feel strengthened, more encouraged and hopeful, as well as deeply loved. You will no longer anxiously crave love. As love comes to you continuously and freely, without you having to perform or compete for it or sustain it, you will experience relief. You will also feel more vibrant, worthy, valued, cared for, respected, satisfied, important, whole, and healed.

In these moments of deeper connection, realize that nothing good is being withheld or denied you by God. You will experience God as the good father He really is, who wants to bless you with good things and make you feel loved, protected, cared for, provided for, happy, and fulfilled. Further, you will feel comforted and reassured, because you realize you are not alone. In a deeper relationship with the Father, you will experience what real love feels like and will never go hungry and thirsty for love again. You won't crave love so much or be so preoccupied with chasing after love from another. God's love will make you feel complete, whole, wanted, and good enough.

Wait patiently, feeling satisfied and deeply loved in your relationship with God the Father and your Lord Jesus. Welcome this opportunity to deepen and strengthen your bond with them, which will impact every area of your life with overflowing love. I encourage you to listen to music and offer Him praise now.

Today's Powerful Thought
I can experience what real love feels like during praise and worship because it deepens my relationship with God and Jesus.

Prayer
Abba Father, help me to experience Your love for me more intimately when I praise and worship in song and by listening to music. Please open my heart to receive Your rich love. Let Your love permeate my entire being so that all my anxieties and fears will be washed away, as I experience just how deeply I am loved and acknowledged by You, as Your child. Help me to become more aware of Your presence and to experience the warm, comforting compassion You offer me each moment I live. I offer You this time right now, so I may rest in Your warm embrace and let myself experience Your genuine, complete, perfect love. Thank You, Abba, that Your love is the ultimate gift of love. In Jesus I pray. Amen.

DAY 9

GREAT EXPECTATIONS: SAYING THANK YOU WHEN GOD SENDS THE UNEXPECTED

Have you ever been in a position where you longed and hoped for something, and when you finally actually received it, you were disappointed to discover that it was not what you had expected? Often, you may pray and then be disappointed when you don't get exactly what you asked for. You may think it can't be the answer that God would provide. You will often discover that the gift you receive from God may be quite different than what you would have chosen yourself. Therefore, don't be surprised if His selection for your husband is quite different than you had expected. How do you appreciate and respect God's selection for you when it is different from what you expected and not exactly what you had wanted? How do you value what you have received?

Common sense says ask God for His confirmation that this is indeed His choice for you. Also, ask for wisdom about what kind of relationship this is meant to be. Meaning, ask if this is a friend, a brother in Christ, or the answer to your prayers for a mate. Be patient in letting God's answer unfold. Most of all, remember to exercise faith. Once you have received His confirmation, that this is His answer, accept it and be satisfied. If you feel disappointed, allow yourself to express this openly to God. It is no surprise to God that you may feel disappointed or struggle with the answer. Allow Him to help you mature spiritually, and to provide His love, compassion, kindness, comfort, wisdom, and guidance. However, don't try to manipulate or press for your own way and desires. Perhaps you have reasonable doubts and don't truly understand His ways and plans. If so, ask God for wisdom and patience, as the relationship develops. Don't be hasty or over-reactive. Ask to be able to value and respect this special person God has selected. As you both develop and heal, ask God to help you see the positive qualities God sees in this person, and the reasons you make a good match.

Let yourself embrace the special quality gift this person is to your life. Allow yourself, with gratitude, to open your heart to this quality person who God has sent to you, no matter the role he will play in your life. If God's answer is to love one another and receive the benefit of brotherhood and friendship only, don't ask for it to be more or strive to push for more. The key is to take the position of appreciation and gratitude for this friend and brother. Ask God for wisdom and help in being fully satisfied with His choice.

You never have to fear who God sends. It will always be for your benefit and good. You can trust Him. God does not compromise on quality. Be fully satisfied with His choice of whether this person is a friend and brother or your future mate. Ultimately, you will offer each other love and support, and help each other grow and learn. Wait in patience to discover who this person really is. Don't rush, push, or try to prematurely accelerate the relationship. Allow both yourself and this person to be free to bloom into who God has made each of you to be. Take time to discover who the other really is. Be patient as deeper love, emotional intimacy, and trust develop. Over time, you will learn to appreciate what makes him uniquely special. Then you will understand and enjoy why God chose him as His best for you. Allow yourself to be fully satisfied with who this person is rather than focusing on things that may be relatively insignificant.

Don't make him try to earn your love or prove he is good enough to receive it. Rather, seek to discover who he is. Learn to appreciate what makes him God's choice for you. Love is a free gift. It is bestowed freely without demand or effort on the part of the bestower. Turn to God continually for help with seeing him the way God sees him and in appreciation of his special and unique qualities, which are beautiful, hidden treasures that complement and enhance who you are and add value to your life in general.

Remember, you don't ever have to earn or win his love. Instead, ask God to help you appreciate what makes you God's choice for this man. It is a wonderful way to get to know yourself better and to see your own very special and unique qualities from God's loving perspective. This will help you to more fully understand, value, respect, and love yourself more like God does. You will also learn to appreciate how very special you are and how you add value to the lives of others as well. You will mature and heal. The goal is to more lovingly accept who you are and who the other is without putting up walls. The goal is also to do this while more deeply engaging in love. This level of emotional vulnerability may be difficult for you, especially if you have been hurt before. You may fear getting hurt again. To overcome feeling fearful in love, you can choose to turn to God each day for love, security, protection, strength, and support. Acknowledge your fears and talk openly, without reserve, to God about them. Ask Jesus to come to your aid. He is your High Priest, your Savior, and intercessor (Hebrews 4:14–16). You can go to the throne of grace and receive help in times of need. You can be reassured that He will most certainly help you. You can receive help to overcome inevitable triggers, defensive reactions, emotional wounds, and problematic relationship patterns associated with painful past relationships.

You will also find that you will need help managing hurt feelings and toxic relationship patterns which developed as a consequence, so that history does not repeat itself, causing you to sabotage your new relationship. Inevitably, he will hurt you and you will also hurt him (intentionally or unintentionally). Although you may fear getting hurt, hurting each other is an inevitable part of every relationship. The ways you hurt each other will be associated with wounds that need healing and with traits and problematic behavior patterns God wants to help each of you overcome. God will help you overcome these problems and hurt in your spiritual relationship with Him and Jesus. This will require that you turn to God and Jesus, instead of responding in hurt, fear, defensiveness, anger, and retaliation. It also means you have to back away from trying to get back at him, punishing him, and making him work harder and harder to earn your love and forgiveness. And it necessitates turning away from attacking his character, integrity, and worth. When you feel hurt and wounded, you will have to learn to not pull away, withdraw, or sabotage and destroy the relationship. You will have to resist responding by feeling attacked, not valued, unimportant, humiliated, and less worthy of love. Instead, during your most vulnerable moments, you are asked to turn to God for comfort, love, understanding, forgiveness, and help with managing your emotions and actions. Perhaps the greatest challenge which God will need to help you with will be to continue to love more unconditionally and compassionately, with patience, acceptance, and forgiveness.

Learning to let go and forgive may be the greatest lesson of all. You are asked to extend the grace you have received in Christ from God, by being kind, compassionate, and forgiving each other (Ephesians 4:32). You will always need God's help in doing this, and God will always lovingly help you, without judgment and condemnation.

Rather, you are asked to approach this relationship with God maturing your spirit and guiding you each step of the way. You are asked to be patient and trust God, as you and the man you are building a relationship with both grow and mature. At times, you will need to offer this man plenty of grace and love. Likewise, he will also need to do the same for you. During this time, you may wrestle with anxiety. Trust God without doubt and fear. Let Him offer you His love and best solutions. Go to Him to get your needs satisfied in a relationship with Him, versus compromising or reflexively responding in customary ways. Ask God to help you forgive this man's failed efforts, limitations, weaknesses, hurtful actions, and areas of necessary growth and maturity. You don't have to go through this difficult time of transition and maturity by yourself. Look to God to provide love, comfort, wisdom, and healing from emotional and spiritual wounds. God loves you with a love that fully satisfies your every need.

Today's Powerful Thought
I trust God to aid me in my growth, maturity, and appreciation of both myself and His choice for my mate.

Prayer
Blessed Father, help me to clearly know, value, and appreciate who You have chosen to be my mate and husband. Help me to not push him away or punish him for his faults. Help me to see him and myself in the beautiful way You see us both. Help us to appreciate each other's special gifts and characteristics placed within us both by You. Help us to discover how blessed we are to be able to have a relationship with each other. Abba Father, help me to be patient, loving, compassionate, and forgiving. In the case where someone is not chosen by You to be my mate, please help me to discover what type of relationship You have blessed us to have. In Jesus I pray. Amen.

DAY 10

HUNGER FOR LOVE

The intensity with which you desperately feel the need for love may overwhelm and exhaust you in every way possible. The hunger to be loved and cared for by another is absolutely a part of every human experience. It is nothing to deny or to feel ashamed and weak about. In these moments of intense need, all focus and priority will be on drawing love to you. The need may be so intensely felt that the urgency to get it met may feel like a matter of instinctual survival. However, after unfruitful, exhaustive efforts, you may eventually experience fading hope and despair.

One can surmise that since this intense need for love is so germane to human experience, love is indeed necessary for our survival. Love is a basic human need. This is why the need functions on the level of an instinctual drive and feels impossible to deny and resist. Why is the need for love so important for human survival? While engaging in spiritual meditation, the answer came to me by revelation. What you, I, and all human beings are really hungry for is God's love. Experiencing God's love is a necessity, which you may not even be fully aware or conscious of. What we are all really desiring is a relationship with our spiritual

Father. We each need to feel perfectly and unconditionally loved, consistently, without variation. This quality of love will make us each feel whole, complete, satisfied, fulfilled, and worthy. Love defines who you are, contributes to the core of your identity, and provides compassion, comfort, forgiveness, understanding, empathy, faithfulness, hopefulness, belonging, safety, security, protection, stability, purpose, meaning, and a sense of destiny. God's love provides what is essential to your entire being, mind, body, soul, and spirit.

Given how critical love is and the vital role it plays in our life, it only makes perfect sense that God's love is the only love which can provide the consistent, perfect, and unconditional love we each need. In truth, we are craving a bond and relationship, similarly to what Adam once enjoyed with God before he sinned. In reality, it is your God intended nature to be made full and complete in relationship with Him (God). God created man to be in a loving relationship with Himself. When God created Eve, to be a partner for Adam, Adam had already been made complete in God and His unconditional love. Eve was never created to be the source of Adam's unconditional love or to complete Adam. Neither was Adam intended to be her source of completion, wholeness, and unconditional, perfect love. Instead, their bond was intended to be one of partnership, help, and aid to each other (Genesis 2:18). Eve, like Adam, enjoyed a relationship with God, based on His unconditional love for her. She was made whole and complete in her relationship with God. We were never intended to be out of close relationship with God, the source of the love we each need to survive.

When Adam sinned, the bond of close relationship with God was broken. Therefore, mankind suffered from the loss of connection and intimate personal relationship with the only source of the perfect, unconditional love needed to survive. As a result of this loss, an intense need to feel loved was experienced by every person. However, it may not be apparent that who we are so desperately seeking, first and foremost, is God, and not the love and companionship or partnership of another person. We are desperate to experience perfect love in a close relationship with God and this will not be possible until we accept Christ, become one with Him, receive the gift of righteousness through Christ, and a relationship with God is reestablished. It is important to know that it is only through Christ Jesus that you can be reconciled to God (2 Corinthians 5:18). Being one with Christ, you will also be able to relax and approach the throne of grace without fear or intimidation. Instead, you can approach God as His beloved child in Christ.

Until you believe in Christ and establish a relationship with Him and God, you will be mistakenly drawn toward others for fulfillment and joy in the experience of their love. During intensely felt moments of need, your desire, loneliness, craving, and emptiness are all pointing to a most significant spiritual need. The solution points directly to an absence of an unconditional, loving relationship and genuine, intimate connection. While you may be focusing on the lack of and need for a relationship with a companion or mate, this will not satisfy your need. The real nature and substance of your need is for a personal and intensely felt experience of unconditional, perfect love in a personal relationship and connection with God. Yet, in these moments of feeling alone and intensely hungry for love, God may seem so far. In the absence of a personal relationship with Him, you will remain hungry for love, accompanied by a lack of fulfillment and joy, loneliness, and emptiness.

What I discovered is that these feelings of separation from God, and His absence, are the consequence of our distancing from God and self-condemnation, versus Him separating and abandoning and not loving us. For example, when you carry the feelings of condemnation, guilt, and shame, this creates the experience of feeling like there is an uncrossable chasm between you and God. What creates this illusion of God's distance and lack of love for you relates to the condemnation and unforgiveness you feel toward yourself. In these moments, you may likely focus on your own performance, goodness, and how worthy and deserving you feel, based on your own merits and performance and the judgment of others. You may experience a sense of condemnation because of your past sins, mistakes, weaknesses, and failures. You may also feel like you don't qualify to receive God's perfect love. In these moments, it may feel impossible to accept God's grace and to think yourself qualified to receive it. Sometimes, if you have experienced repeated pain and disappointment, you may feel like all the evidence points to God punishing and rejecting you. Therefore, it may be harder to enjoy the experience of God's love, grace, and mercy toward you.

You may even reason that you have to work harder to earn back God's love. You may feel like you don't deserve to be happy. In fact, deep down within your spirit, you may not believe that God will really help you or invest Himself and His resources in your personal well-being and happiness. You may feel like it is much too late for you. You may reason that your past actions and failings only further disqualify you from receiving the love of a good man, one of God's special children. In your heart, you may believe that you have no right to receive someone so special in your life. You may be shocked at how you continue to struggle with thoughts of not receiving God's loving grace. Yes, the spirit of self-condemnation is real! It is also a spirit which tries to deflect your consciousness away from Jesus, God's grace, and the special relationship you now have with God through Christ. Condemnation ultimately makes you feel unloved and unworthy of love.

What may also compromise your experience of God's love is the spirit of unforgiveness toward others. When unforgiveness is present, it has a way of becoming the center of your world and your emotional and spiritual experiences. It contaminates everything. It takes away from your sense of joy, peace, and love in your relationship with God and others. What it also does, almost silently, is make you feel condemned. When you wrestle with unforgiveness, hurt, and anger, it stifles your awareness of love and grace in your life from God. Now, the truth is, when you struggle to forgive, you may also struggle to let grace fully operate in your own life. You may also begin to falsely feel like God's grace is absent from your life and does not apply to you. You may find it becomes increasingly difficult to comprehend the very nature of God's love and grace. You may also reason that since you cannot forgive, then you have violated some grace principle and so you are not qualified to receive grace. Remember, what takes you out of focus on grace, mercy, and forgiveness, will make you feel condemned, disqualified, and distant from your Lord and Savior, Christ, and His finished work on the cross.

What resolves this problem? The solution is to remember that God's love and grace will never be based on your performance and how good you are. By grace you are saved, based on the sacrifice of Jesus, the righteous, perfect Lamb of God. You don't receive grace based on your efforts or you being declared good enough based on the quality of who you are. Grace is a free gift of love from God. Further, you were justified by Jesus allowing for the shedding of His blood and the scourging and punishment of His body, even unto death, in your place. He paid the price that was required for your sins and took your sins into Himself and gave you His righteousness in exchange. Therefore, you have now received the righteousness of God in Christ Jesus (2 Corinthians 5:21). This is what qualifies you for God's blessings, including receiving the love of a good husband and having a blessed and happy life in Christ. This is what gives you emotional and physical health, wholeness, fulfillment, satisfaction, and helps you to enjoy His peace. You have received God's forgiveness by grace and the accomplished work of Jesus on the cross. Yes, your past, present, and future sins are all forgiven. You are forgiven and will never be condemned, once you believe and accept Christ as your personal Lord and Savior. Jesus was already condemned in your place and His righteousness more than outweighed your sins on the scales of justice. Therefore, you can never be condemned once you believe and accept Christ. This is grace.

What can you know for certain then? You already have what you have really been hungry for. You have received God's complete and full love. God and Jesus both love you perfectly and completely. What you may perceive as distance or absence is not real. God is right now close to you with His Son, Jesus, fervently offering you love and restoring your sense of home, belonging, and peace. God longs to comfort you, heal your pain, and bless you. He takes pleasure in providing good things to His children (those who receive His Son Jesus and believe). Focus on this instead of judgment, condemnation, loneliness, and feeling unloved. Focus on the truth you receive in His Word, which confirms how much He unconditionally loves you today. Let go of feeling like you have to earn or win His love and blessings. Let go of all thoughts that accuse you of being disqualified because of every bad thing that you did or that was done to you. God's love, grace, and the sacrifice of His Son free you from condemnation and bring you into the flow of God's abundant blessings. Just focus on this instead of your past. Let go of your past.

Forgive yourself, forgive others, and allow yourself to receive God's love. If you struggle to forgive others, ask God to help you. Give Him your struggle and lay it at the feet of Jesus, asking Him to take it onto Himself and carry the burden for you. Be reassured that what others did to you does not cancel your blessings from God. That would mean that what they did is more powerful than what Christ accomplished on the cross when He was sacrificed for you. It would mean that those you struggle to forgive are more powerful than God and so cancel any blessing God wants to bestow. Now I don't know about you, but that sounds completely absurd! Nothing and no one is more powerful than God. Another obvious truth is that no one can give you what God's love and grace can. Another person's love can never fully satisfy you or make you feel unconditionally loved, deeply understood, accepted, forgiven, whole, and healed.

Here is something you can do right now to deeply experience the love of God. Pray in the Spirit. When you pray in the Spirit (pray in tongues), you will feel God's love for you. When you speak in an unknown tongue (the Spirit), you speak directly to God (1 Corinthians 14:2). Therefore, if you are speaking directly to God, this means that speaking or praying in the Spirit or tongues bring you directly into God's presence. When you get that close to God, you will experience His perfect, unconditional love for you. Pray in tongues and rest in His peaceful, loving presence. Nothing is more powerful than experiencing God's love personally. God's love will give you all you have been seeking.

Today's Powerful Thought
God's love makes me feel unconditionally loved, accepted, forgiven, fulfilled, healed, and whole.

Prayer
Abba Father, please draw near to me and help me to receive that special gift of feeling deeply loved and cared for by You. I sometimes wrestle with the feeling that I don't deserve Your love or Your abundant blessings. Sometimes, I struggle with feeling connected to You. In those moments, I also despair of life itself and lose hopefulness about ever receiving love. I also feel at times like I have forfeited my rights to be blessed. Father, please help me to focus on Jesus and how He was sacrificed, so I would no longer ever have to be punished or condemned for my sins, mistakes, and past. Help me to focus on Your love, grace, mercy,

and forgiveness. Please, Father, help me to focus on how much You love me and want to bless me each day I live. Thank You that in You I can live a happy and full life, focusing on Your love and the gift of grace. Please, Father, help me to forgive myself and to forgive others who have wronged me. Help me to give You my burden of unforgiveness. Help me in moments of weakness to turn to You. In Jesus I pray. Amen.

DAY 11

WAITING IN GRATITUDE

In the time of waiting, it can be very difficult to concentrate on anything except on what you lack and don't presently have. The time of waiting, though difficult, is a time of growth and preparation. It is also a time of getting your life, priorities, and sense of purpose and direction on track. A time of waiting brings the opportunity for developing intimacy with God, healing, and discovering who you really are. Instead of becoming impatient or overwhelmed by negativity, you may receive this time with gratitude.

Yes, an attitude of gratitude during the period of waiting is essential for many reasons. One of the most important being that it gives you the distraction-free time needed to connect with God to receive the unconditional love you have been hoping to receive from others. Naturally, a time of waiting helps you to more fully experience God's presence and to reach for Him, instead of others, to satisfy your needs and desires. An attitude of gratitude helps you to shift your focus on appreciating the life, liberty, grace, and love you have received in Christ. It helps you to appreciate your relationship with God, as His child, and your new identity in Christ. It orients you to being more grateful for who and what you presently have in your life. It is also knowing that no matter what the circumstances look like presently, things will eventually get better because God loves you and will help you.

When you focus on your loving relationship with God and how He is presently blessing you, this helps you to know with faith and confidence that God the Father can be trusted and that no good thing will He deny you. When you have an attitude of gratitude, you are better able to establish a position of absolute trust and confidence in God, your Father, to bless you abundantly, protect you, and provide everything you need. This helps you to more deeply operate in faith.

With a thankful attitude you can receive this period of waiting in confident faith and trust that it is for your good and best for you at this present time. Therefore, during this period, walk even more closely with God the Father and seek to see His many blessings which unfold every day in your life. Wake each day of this waiting period with hopeful expectation of receiving blessings, a life of good things, and a good future. Place your hopefulness on the fact that God's Word promises you exactly this (Jeremiah 29:11). Each day, be thankful for and focus on the value of what you have received. Be sure to say thank you to your Abba Father, God.

Make certain you adopt an attitude of gratitude versus lack during this time. It is so easy to see what is missing or what you want and need. The absence of what you don't yet have can overshadow the beauty of your present experiences and diminish your present joy. Instead of looking at your life with a lack mentality, look closely with thankfulness and appreciation for what you do have now.

Seek to actively engage in the present with gratitude and appreciation for the people in your life, the blessings you can enjoy today, and the opportunities currently available to you. Look into the loving faces of the people who are kind, compassionate, and affectionate. Lovingly appreciate those friends, family members, mentors, health workers, and the kind strangers you meet along your life path. Cherish the bountiful blessings God has given you this day to enjoy, take care of your needs, and provide you with comfort and security. Enjoy the positive experience of feeling richly loved and provided for by your Father, God. Remember, many of the things you receive may come by way of human hands, but if you look with spiritual eyes you will see the hand of God behind it all. Also, take pleasure in appreciating and saying a kind word to those who add value and quality to your life.

In this time of waiting, refocusing your perspective is less difficult if you engage in intentional thanksgiving and praise worship. The Word of God which you speak and the praise you offer do make a positive difference in your emotions, mind, thoughts, beliefs, body, and spirit. What you will receive when you engage in thanksgiving, prayers of appreciation, praise, and worship is a powerful transformation that is derived from drawing closer to God. You will feel His presence and love more, and become more consciously aware of how He is powerfully working in every area of your life. You will perceive how He is at work for your protection, good, and benefit. Your enhanced sense of His presence provides joy, peace, and comfort, as well as the reassurance that everything will eventually be okay.

Further, the quality of the words you speak, along with praise and worship in the form of song and music, will enhance your mood and make you appreciate your life and blessings. The words you speak will help to frame the personal experience of your life, who you are, and how satisfied and happy you feel. Words of praise, gratitude, and appreciation that you speak can provide you with hope, even in the most distressing times. The words you speak will also help you build faith as you approach each day with a grateful heart. We are each urged to, with gratitude in our hearts, sing psalms, hymns, and spiritual songs to God and in everything give thanks to God (Colossians 3:16–17). What this suggests is that thanksgiving praise provides a way to more deeply experience hopefulness, peace, and the love of God. It protects against strife, unforgiveness, destructive passions, desires, negative emotions, hopelessness, and impulsive actions.

Take the grateful approach of also thanking God for what you do not yet have but which, through Him, you hope to receive, including the gift of a husband. Yes, thank Him for the very thing you have not yet received in the natural, but which you are hopeful for by faith. Thank Him for answering your prayers even before what you have prayed for manifests in your life. See it as already accomplished and say it is accomplished by God. Only speak words of affirmation by faith and praise God. Your faith and praise move God in powerful ways.

David was very aware of how faith, praise, and worship are beneficial when believing in God for something or facing challenges. He suggested that you do as he did and see powerful results, which he certainly enjoyed in his own life. He suggested that you, like him, bless the Lord at all times, praise Him continually with your mouth, glorify Him, magnify Him, and exalt His name (Psalm 34:1–3). As a result, David said (and his life demonstrated this), you can expect the Lord to answer your prayers and petitions, calm your fears, deliver and save you from every trouble, and offer you a place of refuge (Psalm 34:4–8). What this demonstrates is the power of operating in faith, and offering praise to God and thankfulness, even for what you have not yet received or been delivered from.

Your faith has great power. It produces great things, including miracles, and causes the impossible to come to pass (Mark 10:52, Mark 11:22). Your faith moves God, and, in fact, without faith it is impossible to please Him (Hebrews 11:2, Hebrews 11:6). You are also told that God rewards those who seek Him with an attitude of faith (Hebrews 11:6). What is an attitude of faith exactly? It is having the confidence and certainty that what you hope for will happen and the conviction that what is not seen nor has materialized as yet will one day manifest in your natural or physical reality (Hebrews 11:1). In fact, God demonstrated that when you combine faith with the words you speak, you can bring things into existence.

He did this when He made the worlds. By faith, the worlds were prepared by the Word of God (Hebrews 11:3). What this means is that by His faith combined with His Words, God brought the worlds into physical being. God, by faith, spoke the worlds into existence, so operate in faith and offer thankful praise punctuated with words of faith about receiving what you most want and desire, according to God's will, purpose, and plan for your life. See it as done and visualize what you hope for. Say it is done. Use words based on faith, which confess that it will happen, that God will bring it to pass, and that it is already done by God in the spiritual reality. Declare it is accomplished in Christ and make sure to not speak words of negativity and loss of hope. Align your behaviors with your faith. Make preparations and plans to get ready for what you have prayed for and hope to receive in faith.

Here I must acknowledge the importance of always honoring God's will and wisdom over your own. It is important to submit to His will, plans, and purpose. Let His wisdom inform and direct you. Pray to be in agreement with His will for your life and ask for His imparting of wisdom in this area. Also, relinquish control. The powerful acknowledgement is that God's will is best for you, even if it is not exactly what you wanted or hoped for. Express gratitude to God for giving you His best, doing what is best for you, protecting you, and blessing you. Thank Him for His wisdom and direction.

By being thankful and offering praise to God, you are resting in Him and allowing Him to take control over your circumstances. You are permitting God to bless you in His way and His timing, without you having to work so hard to make things happen. You are also allowing God to operate in your life. Your praise and thankfulness say, "Thank You, God, for what I have and what I will receive by faith." It says, "I trust You, God, to receive the promise without having to orchestrate everything on my own." It says, "I know You love me, Father, and always give me what is best for me." Your attitude of gratitude says, "Thank You, God, for being a good Father to me." It sees the good things God offers you each day and allows you to enjoy them with appreciation and joy, knowing you are loved, cared for, and well provided for by God Himself.

Today's Powerful Thought
Thank You, Father, for all of the bountiful blessings I have already received and the ones I count on receiving in the future.

Prayer

Thank You, Father, that Your promises to Christ are now for me also. Thank You for all of Your bountiful blessings, protection, provisions, and love. I receive them in faith. Praise God! I count on You, God, always, to give me the best. It will happen. Thank You, Father. I receive Your gift of love. Help me to be satisfied with what I have already richly received from You. When I look at the special people I have received in my life and the many blessings I have, I feel so grateful. Thank You that You will provide me with special people in my life, including special friends, beloved family members, and a mate. I am thankful that You never fail to offer me more than I would ever deserve, based on my own merits and efforts. Thank You that through Your grace and the sacrifice of Your Son, Jesus, I benefit from having all the favor, protection, and provisions that Christ qualifies for. Thank You for the blessings I have yet to receive, which I have prayed for. Let it all be according to Your will and perfect time. I am grateful I will receive the gift of a mate. I love You, Father. Thank You for the gift of Your love for me. In Jesus I pray. Amen.

DAY 12

YOUR THOUGHT LIFE

In matters of love, intense and overwhelming emotions can interfere with developing a healthy and lasting relationship. This is especially so when you experience negative emotions, such as anxiety, fear, shame, guilt, and sadness. Negative emotions impact your ability to experience love, function effectively, and also your capacity to interact with others in healthy, positive, and productive ways. Your negative emotions can cause you to feel like you are being tossed to and fro in a whirlwind of doubts, fears, and diminishing hope. When it comes to matters of the heart, you may feel like you are being sucked into a vortex of emotional turbulence.

In the midst of this emotional vortex, it is better to pause and not get sucked into the distressing emotional experience. You may do this by refocusing your thoughts. Negative emotions signal the presence of problematic thoughts and beliefs. Whether or not you are aware of the presence of your problematic thoughts and beliefs, what you are thinking triggers intense emotions and reactions. Negative emotions are red flags, which signal the presence of self-defeating and often erroneous thoughts and beliefs about yourself, others, and your future. The value of knowing this is that it points directly to a positive solution. By altering your problematic thoughts and beliefs, you can change your emotional state. Considering that your faulty thoughts and beliefs sabotage your ability to form lasting, loving relationships, by applying the solution of adjusting your thoughts, you can have a more positive relationship experience.

What you may also likely struggle with is knowing how to do this, especially in the presence of already existing negative emotions and problematic situations. The solution lies in becoming more consciously aware of what you think and believe. Don't assume you know. You may discover that your thoughts, which influence your problematic responses and self-defeating moods, are operating on a semi-conscious level. They are continuously present and sometimes operate on quiet mode in the background. This does not mean, however, that they are not powerful or exercising control over your emotions, actions, choices, relationships, and spiritual life. Basically, they influence the quality of your life.

One thing you can do right away, to refocus or shift your thoughts, is to tune into your emotional experiences in the moment and query them. This slows down the negative emotional cycle and gives you a chance to intervene. This alters the typical course of your negative emotional and behavioral cycle. If possible, in the moment, try to explore the thoughts and beliefs your emotions are connected to. Ask yourself questions. What am I really thinking to myself right now? What are the beliefs that come to mind right now? What conclusions may I be drawing?

What do I imagine are the judgments of others and God? What are the thoughts and beliefs that inform and justify what I am feeling? What am I thinking about myself, others, and my future? What am I thinking about God in general? What do I believe God feels and thinks about me, my situation, my concerns and problems, my behaviors, my past, and my future? Do I feel that this is what I deserve? Do I believe I have hope or a second chance? Focus on what you may be thinking and believing in connection to love. What are your thoughts about your value, worth, and being loved by others, including God? Consider your thoughts and beliefs about the possibility of you receiving the love of a mate. What thoughts keep you feeling burnt out, discouraged, sad, anxious, and defeated? What are you thinking about in terms of being able to move positively forward in establishing and participating in a healthy and loving relationship with a man? What are your fears, anxieties, and worries? What makes you feel hopeless? What do you really believe about your future and your likelihood of enjoying a beautiful and positive relationship with a partner? What are your thoughts and beliefs related to failure, guilt, and condemnation? Who may you be struggling to forgive? What are your thoughts about forgiveness? Do you think God cares about you or loves you?

Once you have discovered the thoughts and beliefs present, you must further examine them for accuracy. What or who supports these thoughts and beliefs? On what foundation and whose word are they based? Let God's Word offer you the firm foundation on which to determine whether your thoughts are true, accurate, and quality, or whether they are false, inaccurate, untrue, not quality, and detrimental to your life.

What you will discover is that you have many core problematic thoughts and beliefs, which influence your mood, your perception of your worth and value and the quality of your life in general. Perhaps you have heard it said that the real battle is for your mind. This simply means that Satan launches his fiery darts by attacking and influencing your thoughts and beliefs (Ephesians 6:16). This is the same method of attack he used when he tempted Jesus (Luke 4:1-13). When tempted, Jesus demonstrated the strategy you can use to defeat thoughts and beliefs that are inaccurate, wrong, and not based on the Word of God, or, in many cases, are contrary to God's Word, nature, and promises. What Jesus did was quote the Word of God. He said, "It is written," whenever tempted by Satan's attack on His mind (thoughts and beliefs). Jesus quoted directly from the scriptures (the Bible). Your emotions are signals that alert you to the quality of your thoughts and beliefs. Basically, negative and toxic emotions are signals that alert you to the fact that something is wrong with your thought life. Your negative emotions are often in response to your problematic, toxic, and wrong thoughts and beliefs.

If your thoughts are not based on God's Word, then you will likewise experience negative, toxic, crippling, and debilitating emotions. When you change the quality of your thoughts and align them with God's Word, and the truth about His promises, His love for you, His protection, and your worth and value in Christ, then your emotions will improve, as will the quality of your behaviors, relationships, and life in general. During moments when you experience toxic, negative emotions, refocus your thoughts on the Word of God, which directly addresses the areas of toxic, problematic thinking or the associated problematic, toxic emotions you are experiencing. For example, if you find yourself feeling fearful about a situation in your life, then consider what it says in 2 Timothy 1:7: "For God has not given us the spirit of fear but of power, of love, and of a sound mind."

In fact, keep repeating the written Word out loud. The Word of God, which you hear (even as it is spoken out loud to yourself or another), edifies your spirit and builds your faith (Romans 10:17). You can also listen to and read God's Word from a minister God leads you to. Use God's Word to replace problematic, inaccurate, and wrong thoughts and beliefs. If you fear that you will never be loved, but instead live a life of being isolated and uncared for, speak God's Word out loud and correct the thoughts. Focus instead on the words of the scripture about how much God loves you and about His promises to bless you. If you also feel hopeless and dejected because you struggle with this thought, actively refocus. Acknowledge your feelings, identify the associated problematic, negative or toxic thoughts and beliefs, and then turn to God's Word to see what His promises are for your life. Focus on the love, grace, and favor He has toward you as a saved child of the Most High King. Read scriptures about His promises, such as that no good thing will He deny you when you walk with Him and that His promises are yes in Christ (Psalm 84:11, 2 Corinthians 1:20). If you connect with feeling guilty, ashamed, depressed, and hopeless about your future, because you have sinned and made many mistakes or feel too old, it is not too late for you to have your second chance. Jesus was sacrificed in your place so that you could enjoy a second chance. Remember that, "God's grace was given to us in Christ Jesus before the ages began" (Timothy 1:9, John 1:16–17). God loves you so much He sacrificed His Son for you (John 3:16). Christ the Lord loves you so much that He allowed Himself to take the punishment for your sins so that you could be set free and live a new life. Therefore, you have complete forgiveness of sins and can never be condemned once you are in Christ (Romans 8:1–2). Jesus is your guarantee of God's grace and favor.

Continuously focus on the favor and blessings you benefit from, because you are a joint heir with Christ and a child of God (Romans 8:15–17). You have received the righteousness of God through Christ and are one with Him (2 Corinthians 5:21). Further, Jesus promised that if you believe, remain in Him, and His Words remain in you, then you will receive whatever you asked for, because the Father loves to give good gifts to you, His child (Mathew 21:22, Mathew 7:7–11, John 15:7). Jesus stated that it was to the glory of God that you should bear much fruit (John 15:8). Realize, therefore, that God's glory is demonstrated through you, the richness of His blessings granted to you, and the full quality life He offers you. He blesses you as a testimony of His great love, grace, and mercy. Not surprisingly then, your life is destined for better, actually for God's absolute best, to His glory! Focus on scripture that talks about the overflowing favor and blessings you receive by grace from God, who loves to richly provide us with everything for our enjoyment (Jeremiah 29:11, 1 Timothy 6:17). Acknowledge that God will supply all your needs according to His riches in glory in Christ Jesus (Philippians 4:19). What a beautiful thing to know that you don't have to worry or fear because God takes care of your needs and provides got you. Included in God's provision are His promises of protection for you (Psalm 91). What all of this confirms is that you have incredible worth and value, which you have received in Christ. You are loved, special, and important to God, who demonstrated this by the sacrifice of His own Son, Jesus, for you. Therefore, you never need to question your worth and value again or worry about receiving provision, protection, and blessings, including the blessing of a partner.

Consider then how powerfully you can use the spirit of self-discipline and a sound mind, which you received from God, to actively focus on the Word of God in exercising control over your thought life and beliefs, as well as the words you speak (2 Timothy 1:7, the New Revised Standard Version translation uses the words self-discipline). You can absolutely challenge those toxic and problematic thoughts, which manipulate your emotions, behaviors, relationships, and the quality of your life, by focusing on the Word of God, His love for you, His grace, your righteous identity through Christ, God's provision, His protection of you, and everything you are and will receive as a child of God. You are destined to live a quality life and receive God's best.

Today's Powerful Thought
I will focus my thoughts and spoken word on the Word of God to defeat negative emotions and problematic beliefs, behaviors, and relationship patterns.

Prayer
Father, thank You for comforting me in times of deep emotional distress and for anchoring me in Your Word,

so that I may adjust the quality of my thinking and believe the right thing about my life, Your love for me, Your protection, and the favor I receive through my relationship with You and Jesus. I am thankful that I am Your child. Help me to reflect on Your love for me, Your promises of abundant blessings, and Your grace and forgiveness. Help me to remember that Jesus already paid the price for my sins. Thank You for helping me to change my wrong beliefs by allowing Your Word to saturate my mind and spirit. Help me to continue to focus on the quality life I receive in Your Son and the righteousness which I have received through Him. Thank You that I can live my best life yet and enjoy love in a relationship with You, and eventually in a quality relationship with a mate. In faith I receive it. In Jesus' name I pray. Amen.

DAY 13

MY BEST FRIEND, JESUS

You know that friend?
Who lights up when you walk in
That smile that can't be suppressed
That emanates from deep within
Whose Spirit draws you near
And reassures you are always welcome here
Who is always glad you came?

Most assuredly that most treasured friend is Jesus. Jesus is that friend, brother, protector, close confidant, and guide we all wish for. He is your merciful Savior who allowed Himself to be sacrificed so that you would not be judged and punished for your sins. By God's grace, your sins are forgiven through Jesus. You can always call on Jesus, who welcomes you, and never fails to answer and receive you with warmth, kindness, compassion, and love. He celebrates when you come to Him and is ready to listen with His heart. He never shames, judges, condemns, or criticizes. He always encourages and wants the best for you. His listening heart is receptive to your cries for love, acceptance, forgiveness, comfort, empathy, compassion, and understanding. He offers you help, guidance, and wisdom. He carries your burdens and strengthens you. He is your safe place of protection, peace, and rest.

When you go to Jesus, you never have to suppress who you are or what you truly feel. You never have to hold back the things that are essential about you. When you are feeling lonely and wanting to feel loved, there is no better place to go than to spend time with Jesus. His love is like a healing, warm glow of light that embraces you tenderly and regenerates you. In His presence, you experience peace, mercy, and grace. In His light, you experience hope. When you have an ongoing relationship with Jesus, you find yourself being transformed in His image, from one degree of glory to another (2 Corinthians 3:18). The more you focus on Jesus, the more you find yourself being transformed. You experience new life and freedom in the spirit (2 Corinthians 3:17). It is like being loved back into existence. You feel whole, complete, protected, healed from your brokenness, and unconditionally loved.

Call out His name when you are struggling with needing to feel loved, wanted, desired, and good enough. He will come instantly. I have never been disappointed in His immediate response or the quality of the experience of being in His presence. I have felt completely and unconditionally loved. Just try it. I promise you will not be disappointed in the love you receive from Jesus. His love is never withheld, and you are always completely acknowledged.

In your relationship with Jesus, what you will experience is that you can pour out your soul and always feel deeply listened to, empathized with, understood, care for, comforted, encouraged, and unconditionally loved. In your need and hurt, you can tell Him all your secrets and let Him know the desires of your heart. I have grown so accustomed to pouring out my heart and coming fully into Jesus' presence with all my worries, troubles, concerns, disappointment, mistakes, confusion, despair, hopes, dreams, anxieties, fears, condemnation, shame, guilt, sadness, grief, and hopelessness. He never grows tired of me. With Jesus, what you will experience is Him tenderly drawing you nearer and creating a sense of inner peace, which flows from Him. His presence also communicates a sense of protection and strength. As you focus on Jesus and experience His presence, you feel more worthy, valued, and good enough.

What eventually develops, as a result, is a genuine feeling of self-love, as you begin to recognize yourself as a reflection of Jesus (2 Corinthians 3:18). You will internalize the experience of being one with Him, someone who is no longer condemned, but instead loved and righteous through Him (2 Corinthians 5:21). In other words, when you are in relationship and connection with Jesus, your internal experience of who you now are in Christ (a new, righteous creation) becomes more real and deeply felt. You experience feeling worthy in your connection with Him. Yes, you will absolutely have a love experience in your relationship with Jesus. Remember, you are one with Christ and so have received His Spirit and righteous identity (1 Corinthians 6:17, Romans 7:4, Romans 8:9). What you experience is the presence of Him in you, and the presence of the Spirit and glory of God

(2 Corinthians 3:18). What you also receive is the experience of yourself as genuinely beautiful and loved in His presence.

In a relationship with Jesus, you learn to accept His love, as well as God's love, more deeply than ever before. You realize that genuine love is beautiful in your relationship with Jesus and God. The experience of such a deeply fulfilling, complete, and satisfying, perfect love creates the space for you to genuinely love others and recognize, invite, and accept genuine love from others. You also realize and believe that love is possible between yourself and a mate. This is all because you experience feeling genuinely, perfectly and completely loved, accepted, and cared for, not based on your performance or some other criteria. You will never have to do anything to deserve Jesus or God's love ever.

In the midst of every storm, Jesus draws nearer to you. You can depend on Him to come when you are in need. He provides shelter, protection, loving comfort, peace, and His strength from which to draw from. You can trust and confide in Him. He is your best friend who always listens with love and understands. He offers you help and lets you know you can depend on Him no matter what. He is your partner, who is always there to provide what you lack and need. He provides the strength you need to face challenges and in your weakest moments or when you feel overwhelmed. You can look to Jesus to provide His never-ending supply of love, provision, protection, strength, and everything you need. He is the friend who gives freely, by grace, and never asks you to repay Him. You can rest in Him.

You can also depend on Jesus to help you make good decisions and to follow the path and plan God intends for your life. When you feel torn between the desires of your flesh and the Spirit, or confused and need assistance with walking in the Spirit and the way of God, let Him guide you and offer you wisdom. Look to Jesus for help in every area of your life and focus on Him, not only during challenges, but also when making important decisions in every area of your life, including in the area of love and marriage. You are encouraged to stay focused on Jesus as Peter was asked to do in the midst of the storm, when he wanted to walk on the water (Matthew 14:29–31). When you don't feel you can persevere, hold on to hope, knowing that Jesus is always there to help you by grace.

Remember, Jesus values and loves you so much, He allowed Himself to be sacrificed for you. He is the "friend who sticks closer than a brother," who is always there for you to depend and lean on forever (Proverbs 18:24). In your relationship with Him, you will know with certainty that you are truly loved, cared for, and favored by Him and God. Simply remember this. Jesus is always on your side. God is always on your side. God has also appointed Jesus as your High Priest and intercessor, who appeals to the Father on your behalf (Hebrews 7:23-27, Romans 8:34). How wonderful it is to live each day receiving love, protection, and provision without having to earn it, compromise yourself to receive it, or live in fear of it leaving.

Today's Powerful Thought
Jesus is my best friend and Savior, who loves me unconditionally, welcomes me with joy, and offers help, grace and His abundant supply of everything I need.

Prayer

Jesus, I call on You now to come close to me. Please help me feel Your Spirit, Your presence, and, most of all, Your love. Help me through these difficult times and my time of waiting to receive a partner who loves me the way You do. Help me, Jesus, to not worry or despair of hope. I'm asking for Your love, comfort, understanding, and the benefit of Your wisdom and counsel. Please help me to discern who the right people to connect with are and who to not let close. I ask for Your help in walking in the Spirit and following the path God has set before me. I ask for Your protection from harm. I ask for Your provision and abundant supply of everything I need and lack. Please offer me Your strength and Your listening heart. Help me to feel loved and to experience feeling worthy, accepted, and appreciated. Thank You, Jesus, that You hear me and are near me now. Thank You that You love me. Please help me to rest in the presence of Your peace right now in this beautiful moment with You. Amen.

DAY 14

PRAYING IN FAITH

Did you know that your faith, combined with prayer, will manifest even more of God's favor, blessings, healing, miracles, and help in your life? But how do you unleash this power in your life and in the area of your relationships? It comes down to learning how to put your faith into operation in the area of prayer. You may pray continuously to receive something and keep asking and hoping day after day, without seeing it manifest in your life. It can be tremendously distressing and troubling to the spirit—when you desperately want something and pray for it but do not see it happening. You may falter in being able to maintain a positive expectation and hopefulness when you keep asking but don't see results. Likely, you may become agitated or begin to question if this is meant for you or if God desires to give it to you. You may question whether it is His will.

Feeling despondent, you may try to convince yourself that you are better off without it or that it is too late, and you must resign yourself to not having what you hoped for. On the flip side, like Sarah (Abraham's wife), when she became exasperated after a long period of waiting for the promise, you may doubt God, give up hope, and try to attain it yourself (Genesis 16:1-3). In doing so, you may complicate your life, suffer undesirable consequences, and live outside the will of God for your life. So how do faith and prayer work when you desire to be married to a partner who God has chosen for you?

Jesus advised that you do not fear, knowing that you are valued and cared for by God far beyond what you can imagine (Matthew 10:29-31). Further, Jesus counseled that you should have faith in God that your prayers will be answered, and you will receive what you prayed for (Mark 11:22-24). His definition of faith included not doubting in your heart, but rather believing without doubt that you have received what you prayed for and that it is done (Mark 11:23-24). Faith is further defined as the confidence of things hoped for and the conviction of things not seen (Hebrews 11:1). What this means is that when you pray, you must also believe in faith for what you have prayed for before it manifests or shows up in your life. Faith says you believe God and will not doubt that His will for your life is to bless you with the mate He has chosen for you. By faith you believe in things not seen yet, knowing that God is compassionate and that your faith will result in great reward (Hebrews 10:35).

In prayer, you can ask for help with whatever you struggle with that may interfere with your faith. This includes doubts and fears of being hurt and disappointed if you believe in love again or open up yourself to the hope of having a loving relationship with a mate. You may also not value yourself and fear that you may never be loved and have a good relationship with a mate. You may fear that you are not worthy or good enough and, therefore, you must engage in exhaustive efforts to keep the interest, attention, and love of another. You may even fear eventually losing the love of the one you open up yourself to love. Additionally, you may struggle with desires and lack of control, which often lead to making bad decisions, compromising, and indulgences, which come with painful consequences. Whatever you are struggling with, God already knows. Therefore, in prayer, you need never hide your true self or keep secrets from God. Take the opportunity to ask for God's help and healing. Let Him take care of it.

Trust God to provide the answers and to give you peace of mind and comfort. Ask that His will be done in your life and then release it all to Him. Truly believe that His good for your life will be fulfilled. Trust God and let Him take the lead. This means you will need to allow His wisdom, plans, and timing to take precedence over your own judgment and plans. You can do this, trusting that you will always feel best when you ask for God's help and allow His plans and will for your life. Allow the Holy Spirit to lead you by guiding you to the right people, places, and circumstances at the right time. Which means that you must also allow for God's timing and accept His choices for the right people and circumstances for your life. What this means is also becoming submissive and obedient to His will and wisdom for your life. In prayer, ask for God's help with submitting to His will for your life. Declare in faith that His plans are better than your own and His will is best. Trust that God will do what He said He will do.

Pray in all earnestness to receive a mate whom God has chosen for you—a man who loves you similar to the way that Christ loves you. Pray for someone who believes in and is grateful for the love and grace of God and extends grace and forgiveness to others. Above all, pray that it be done to the glory of God and not based on selfish need and desire. Pray that your marriage demonstrates God's love, grace, and the better life that is in Christ, being one with Him. Pray that your life, your partner's life, and your marriage serve as a testimony of the love, grace, and glory of God for the good of others.

Pray believing in your heart that God is able and willing to do all that you have asked. Do this knowing you have received the grace, favor, and love of God. Do it knowing your sins are forgiven because of the sacrifice of Jesus, thereby knowing that in Christ you are a new creation and are righteous through Him and now a child of God (2 Corinthians 5:17, 2 Corinthians 5:21, 2 Corinthians 6:18, Galatians 3:26). Also, pray knowing that God desires to bless you and grant you good things, hope, and a good life and future (Jeremiah 29:11).

Further, in prayer, ask Jesus to make intercession for you to Abba Father, God. Jesus is your High Priest, seated at the right hand of the Father, who empathizes with you, petitions the Father on your behalf, and makes intercession for you in all things (Romans 8:34, Hebrews 4:15, Ephesians 1:20–23). Jesus knows exactly what to express on your behalf and what to ask for, even when you struggle with knowing how to pray, what to ask for, and how to express what you really feel. You are encouraged to approach God's throne of grace with confidence, knowing that you will receive love, grace, understanding, compassion, and help with your every need (Hebrews 4:16). Therefore, know that God will respond to your prayers in your time of need. He will do this because He loves you, willingly gave up His own Son for you, and graciously gives you all things (Romans 8:32).

After you have prayed, thank God for listening and providing the answers. Offer prayers of thanksgiving to God in faith.

Thank Him for accomplishing it all by His strength, in His perfect time, and in His way, all to His glory. Thank Him for supplying all your needs according to His riches in glory, as it is written in His Word (Philippians 4:19). Praise Him continuously that it is a finished work through Him, by grace, and through Jesus. Stop praying over and over again, where you are begging, pleading, and requesting the same thing. Believe that God heard you the first time and has already provided the solution. Believe in faith that God works for your good.

Faith means to hope and believe without seeing (Hebrews 11:1). This means you have to hope, believe, and behave like your answer is provided and all is well with you, even before you see it all take place in your life. Like the Shunammite woman whose son died and knew that Elisha could heal him, when asked how her son was doing, you, like her, must confess and declare, "It is well" (2 Kings 4:26). She focused on what she believed God is able and willing to do and not on her present circumstances or on her worthiness and performance. Her spoken words aligned with what she believed about God. This is faith in practice. In your own walk of faith, you must declare and confess in your prayers, your private thoughts, self-talk, and conversations with others that all is well because God has answered your prayer and is able to do it all. He is your good Father who blesses you and protects and provides for you.

When you pray, realize that you can anchor your faith in Jesus. He is the author and perfecter of faith (Hebrews 12:2). Therefore, you can be confident that you can endure anything and receive protection, blessings and favor, because Jesus is the originator of faith and completes your faith. His faith is capable and has endured and overcome on your behalf. His faith provides what you lack by grace, in every area of your life. Simply trust Jesus to sustain you and supply whatever faith you need. He is able to help you in the area of believing for a blessing and maintaining faith.

What else do you need to know about Jesus' faith? He has perfect faith. We are told that through the grace that is in Christ, everyone who is one with Christ receives the measure of faith (Romans 12:3). You do not have to struggle or qualify to receive this gift of faith. It is freely given to every believer. What this simply means is that your faith is derived from the perfect faith of Christ. This is the exceptional quality of the faith God has given you. You have received the measure of the perfect faith of Christ. Walk in His perfect faith when you experience various trials or when praying to receive God's blessings, protection, and favor. Let your thoughts, behaviors, and spoken words reflect Christ's faith. Do it all effortlessly, by grace.

Also, realize that Jesus deserves to receive everything good, because He is perfect and good. He is worthy and righteous and, therefore, deserves every blessing. When you accept Christ as your Savior, you become one with Him and receive His righteous Spirit, being made one with Him (1 Corinthians 6:17, 2 Corinthians 5:21, Romans 7:4). What this means is that by grace you are identified with Christ, therefore, by grace the simple truth is that you will be blessed based on what Christ deserves.

The Lord, Christ Jesus, has the love and favor of God the Father, who has given Him (Christ) His glory and delights in blessing Him. Therefore, expect good things and for your prayers to be answered for your good, because this is what Jesus deserves from the Father. Further, you are a joint heir with Christ (Romans 8:17). You will be blessed by grace based on Jesus' identity, performance, and rightful inheritance.

Another powerful tool, which combines faith and prayer, is praying in the Spirit or tongues (Ephesians 6:18). This is an essential part of being strong in the Lord and a powerful weapon for standing against the devil and whatever struggles you face. Praying in tongues edifies or builds you up (1 Corinthians 14:4). In Latin, the word "edify" means to "construct, strengthen, and build up." This refers to strengthening your dwelling place, which is your body. When your body is strengthened and built up, you become better able to physically take on challenges, bear burdens, withstand, endure, have perseverance, activate miracles in your body, and heal. Your body becomes more powerful. There is also a restorative process that is activated. When you strengthen the body, you are essentially powerfully strengthening and building up your physical temple of the Holy Spirit within you.

Likewise, as you are an interconnected, multidimensional being, your Spirit, mind, and emotions will also benefit and be edified or built up. When you are edified and built up by speaking in tongues, you will also be taught, educated, instructed, counseled, guided, and enlightened morally and spiritually. This means you become knowledgeable and wiser in the things of God. You are also better able to discern God's wisdom and perfect will. Therefore, praying in tongues is a powerful strategy for building up your faith and helping you to stand strong in faith and belief in God, no matter what challenges you face.

As you grow in spiritual understanding of God and His ways, your spirit is built up, becomes stronger, is able to be better guided by God's wisdom, becomes more aware of how God's ways are beneficial and wise, experiences the flow of love and grace from God, and receives counsel, encouragement, comfort, energy, and strength to endure and persevere with patience and love. When you are built up, strengthened, and enlightened in the body and the spirit, you are better able to withstand all the challenges you face, by the power of God's Spirit. By doing this, God is able to help you enter into His rest and not worry, doubt, fear, or become overwhelmed by negative emotions, thoughts, and beliefs (Isaiah 28:11–12). Therefore, you can also experience His peace. In this resting place, God also speaks to His people (Isaiah 28:12). This means that God can impart wisdom, counsel, guidance, and instructions directly to you, which will help you. You don't have to worry or fear because God will impart it all to you while helping you to also feel His peaceful presence.

When you pray in the Spirit or speak in an unknown tongue, you speak directly to God (1 Corinthians 14:2). The ability to have your spirit pray directly to God—when you do not know what to pray for or are uncertain about how you should pray—is also very powerful. The Holy Spirit takes the lead and utters mysteries of the Spirit directly to God. Therefore, you can be reassured that God hears and understands you completely, even when you don't know what is needed or cannot fully understand or express everything yourself.

Prayer in the Spirit sustains you without you having to try to accomplish it on your own. When you pray in the Spirit, you experience a sense of peace and rest. You also experience a sense of harmony and unity with God, Jesus, and the Holy Spirit. In your spirit, you know that all is well and will be done for you. You connect with the feeling of love, grace, life, protection, and provision. All of you more fully embraces being in the Spirit. Surely, knowing that such power flows by praying in tongues, your faith will be strengthened, because you know and feel that God is with you, is working on your behalf, and wishes to strengthen, sustain, and help you in every situation and area of need.

Therefore, pray in faith. Pray in the Spirit. Confess it is done after you pray. Believe that you have received it already. Do not despair; instead see it as done already and focus your prayers on acknowledging this simple truth. Focus on Jesus and the grace and favor you freely receive through your connection and identification with Him. Focus on being loved already. Walk around each day allowing this to occupy your thoughts. Say, "I am loved. I am blessed. I am favored. I am forgiven by grace through Jesus. I will have a beautiful marriage and a life of longevity, full of good days." Declare this by faith when you pray.

Today's Powerful Thought
When I pray in faith, I know that God will provide the answers and blessings by grace. I will pray in the Spirit in faith to fight my battles, and at times when I do not know what to ask for or how I should pray.

Prayer
Dear Abba Father, thank You that You heard my payer. Thank You for Your love and for receiving the gift of grace through the sacrifice of Your precious Son, Jesus. Thank You that I can pray to You in the Spirit to feel Your peaceful presence in times when I am overwhelmed, and do not know what to ask or pray for.

Help me to recall that Jesus is the author and perfecter of my faith. Thank You, Abba Father, for a husband and a marriage that glorifies You and is a testimony of Your love, grace, rich favor toward me, and Your goodness. I declare that what I prayed for is done already through You and that You will provide the answers, blessings, and favor. In the name of Jesus, I pray. Amen.

DAY 15

DEPENDING ON THE SOURCE OF MY FAITH

When you don't have the answer, are facing difficult times, fear, and struggle with faith, go to the ultimate source of your faith—Jesus. Jesus is the author and perfecter of our faith (Hebrews 12:2). This means your faith originates from Jesus. When you are praying for your breakthrough or struggling with a condition, you do not have to go through it alone. As the originator of your faith, Jesus is the source. This simply means that your faith is actually originated from Jesus' faith. Your faith is based on the quality of Jesus' faith.

God loves you so much that He didn't want your faith to be based on your level of strength, effort, fallibility, or perfection. He did not want you to have to struggle to generate your own faith or to maintain it yourself. To everyone, God has given the measure of faith (Romans 12:3). All you have to do is put the faith that you derived from Jesus in action.

God provided the answer to your limitations in activating faith and maintaining faith in Jesus. What does this mean? Since Jesus is the originator of your faith, when faith needs to be activated or maintained, all you have to do is turn to Jesus to evaluate the quality of faith you have been given and what the faith you have been given from Jesus, as the originator, believes and says. Therefore, when you fear, doubt, or struggle, put the faith of Jesus, which you have received, in action, on your behalf.

When your faith wavers or is weak, say to Jesus, "What do you say by faith in this situation or about myself and my condition?" At these times, you can consider what Jesus would say to someone in your situation or if facing a circumstance Himself. You may ask yourself, "What would Jesus' faith say concerning my situation?" Go to the Word of God and see for yourself what Jesus confessed in faith and how He spoke about His faith in God. Use the words Jesus used and say them to yourself and out loud. Let your thoughts and words reflect the words of faith of Jesus. Jesus' faith always says, "My Father, God, loves me. God is able. I believe and do not doubt. He will glorify me so that I may glorify Him. Nothing is impossible with God. Your condition will improve. God will provide." Jesus' faith says, "My Father is able to do this."

Jesus is the originator of your faith, so even if things seem impossible, draw from Jesus' faith to sustain you without you trying so hard. Jesus' faith encourages you and reassures you that you will get through this together with Him, the Holy Spirit, and God. Jesus provides His peace and comfort, along with faith. He provides His faith to be your resource, no matter what you struggle with. Simply focus on Jesus and believe what His faith is able to believe and do.

Today's Powerful Thought
As the originator of my faith, Jesus assures me we will get through this together, that God is able, and all will work out for my good in the end.

Prayer
Thank You, God, for loving me and giving me Jesus as the originator of my faith. Thank You for the quality faith I received from Jesus. Jesus, please reinforce my faith and help me to be stronger in faith by relying on Your perfect faith to help me through difficult times. Give me a sense of peace and harmony with You, Father, Jesus, and the Holy Spirit. I know my condition will improve, because Jesus knows that You, Father, are able to provide all I need. Thank You that I can look to the quality of Jesus' faith to determine the quality of the measure of the faith I have received. By the faith I was given from Jesus, I believe. In Jesus I pray. Amen.

DAY 16

SPIRITUAL WISDOM

When praying for a husband, you must exercise faith. However, your response after prayer is just as important. It is not sufficient to only pray; you must also, afterward, demonstrate faith that your answer will be provided according to the will of God. What this means is your beliefs, thoughts, and behaviors should reflect your confident expectation that it will actually happen according to God's perfect plan, purpose, and timing. You must make a positive confession by faith. By faith you are asked to believe God will provide the answer and it is only a matter of time before it manifests in your life.

Faith hopes and believes without yet seeing (Hebrews 11:1). As Jesus said, "So I tell you, whatever you ask for in prayer, believe that you have received it (**past tense, already accomplished**) and it will be done." (Mark 11:24) In some translations, it says believe you are receiving it (**present tense, now**) and it shall be done. What this means is that you must trust that God has accomplished it for you already.

If you have asked God for permission to get married and His answer is yes, then from that day forward, trust Him at His

Word. Always remember that God is not a man that He should lie (Numbers 23:19). That means, whatever God promised you, He will do it. Whatever He said to you, He will fulfill. God has promised to bless and provide for His children, like a good Father, and simply asks that you not worry, but rather focus on Him, trust, and expect He will supply what you need (Matthew 6:28-34). Nothing is greater than He—not your past, other people, Satan, or problems and challenges. Further, He loves you so much that He sacrificed His own Son to save you (John 3:16-17). Therefore, you can trust God, without any shadow of a doubt, to keep His Word and do what is for your good. Yes, you can always trust God. He has accomplished it for you already.

Therefore, after you pray, thank God for the promise He has accomplished and that will soon come to pass. Allow yourself to dream and envision the promise. For example, see yourself as a partner and a wife. See yourself living side by side as one. Allow yourself to experience the peace that comes from knowing without a doubt that God will provide and bless you. Do not wait until it is fulfilled to speak words of faith. Your faith and belief activate blessings. For without faith, it is impossible to please God (Hebrews 11:6). By faith, many—including Abraham, Joseph, and Moses—believed, were obedient, and, by doing so, received blessings (Hebrews 11:8-30). See it as already being prepared for you and happening. While you wait, speak words of faith, based on the Word of God.

What is also required is your patience. When you believe it will happen, you do not have to panic and try to make it happen on your own or give up and despair. You will not have to manipulate, persuade, or seduce to attain your blessings. Your husband will already be attracted to you and willingly incline his heart to yours. The same will happen for you. You do not have to experience anxiety about whether you may not recognize him when he comes into your life or, more importantly, that you may miss the opportunity. You will not have to see the whole plan and make it all happen. Patience requires that you give God the authority to take the lead and be in charge, to His glory. Let it be all accomplished through Him. Allow Him to manifest it all and allow yourself to benefit from His grace.

Invite God's wisdom. Pray to receive wisdom and then permit God to impart His wisdom to you. Often, anxiety makes you think you have to make rash decisions. Anxiety demands you plan and strategize. Instead, invite God's will to be done. Instead of operating in anxiety, fear, and doubt, allow God to do the work and let it all unfold according to His will. Do not try to control the outcome. Accept whatever God's plan and will is for your life and trust it will all be for your good.

In your prayer and worship life, allow for the opportunity to listen and receive the gift of God's presence and wisdom. Allow Him to guide you in the Spirit by creating a listening space between you and God. Creating a listening and not talking space means trusting God and giving permission for His way and wisdom to be imparted to you. It means connecting by allowing His Spirit to communicate with yours and being open to embracing the full presence of God.

In this space, you are not possessed by His Spirit but, rather, you become one with Him. God's Spirit leads and instructs you. He offers His peace, understanding, compassion, comfort, grace, and love. He provides solutions that are both spiritual and practical. He offers you the opportunity to learn and mature spiritually.

He guides you in your life. This does not have to happen via words communicated directly. In this powerful connection with God, you are engaging your entire self to trust God, flow in unity with His Spirit, and follow His Spirit. In this space, you allow your own spirit to function in unity with God. It is also a posture of stillness in the spirit—where you no longer struggle within to trust, accept God's plan for your life, and follow God's will. You no longer aspire to control the outcome, do it your own way, and follow your own plans and desires. What you will also receive in your spirit is a sense of peace and of being protected and provided for.

Today's Powerful Thought
God's wisdom is always for my best. I will listen and allow God to counsel and guide me in unity with His Spirit, according to His will for my life.

Prayer
(Find a quiet place free of distractions
today before you start this prayer.)
Dear Abba, in times of struggle and impatience, help me to feel Your love and know You want me to have blessings, health, provision, peace, and happiness. Thank You that it is Your will to offer me wisdom, guidance, and blessings. Help me to rely on the benefit of Your wisdom and guidance. Help me to focus on Your Son, Jesus, and His finished work on the cross which by grace made us one and entitles me to every blessing

and good thing I ask for, according to Your will and for Your glory. Praise God! Father, thank You for Your answered prayers. It is accomplished in Christ. May my life and my relationship with my future husband glorify You and be directed by Your wisdom and Your plans for our lives. I lean in to listen and not speak right now as I ask You to help me create the space to receive Your wise counsel. Please lead me step-by-step today. I open my heart and spirit to Your presence and to listen, because I know You love me and always want what is best for me. In the name of Jesus I pray. Amen.

DAY 17

WILLINGNESS TO CHANGE

In truth, you must be willing to also change, learn, grow, and shift from your customary habitual system of beliefs, thoughts, and behaviors in order to receive the promise. You may be focusing on the wrong question. It is not a question of whether God will bless you, but rather one of whether you are ready to receive the promise. If you were to go into a relationship with your customary patterns and habitual beliefs, thoughts, and behaviors, then likely your new relationship would suffer.

Are you ready for a relationship with your partner and mate? Are you willing to make the changes God is leading you to make? Are you willing to learn, grow, and mature spiritually? Are you willing to endure and grow deeper in faith, hope, love, empathy, commitment, faithfulness, understanding, acceptance, compassion, and forgiveness? Are you willing to go through life's journey with someone else—to change, learn, grow, and mature together? Are you willing to accept the gift of God's wisdom and guidance? Are you willing to rest in the finished work of Jesus on the cross and benefit from His sacrifice for you? Are you willing to let God be in control?

Despite your struggles and difficult history, you can still experience a beautiful, loving relationship with a person of quality. However, one of the things that must change along the path of maturity relates to your struggles in your relationship patterns. One key change involves learning to become more emotionally vulnerable and present with others. This involves being more fully engaged, less guarded and defensive, more spontaneous, natural, honest, and genuine, and more deeply emotionally intimate and open with another person. You must also become more comfortable with being in a real relationship that reflects mutual full engagement, respect, validation, warmth, compassion, support, understanding, empathy, acceptance, forgiveness, commitment, faithfulness, and love.

For your relationship to be healthy and thrive, your relationship environment cannot be inhospitable. Neither you or your potential partner will survive where bitterness, anger, unforgiveness, defensiveness, invalidation, dishonesty, distrust, fear, jealousy, struggles for control and power, disrespect, lack of emotional intimacy, and lack of deep consideration, compassion, and kindness exist between both of you. If your relationship environment is unhealthy, then both of you will be deeply wounded, and the relationship will become toxic, and likely not last.

It is not advisable to wait until you are in a relationship or until a crisis unfolds before making changes and learning new patterns of thoughts, beliefs, and behaviors. It is best to make a commitment to learning, maturing, and making personal changes prior to committing your life to another. It is important to establish better and healthier patterns and behaviors, as well as shifts in your beliefs and thoughts, prior to starting a new relationship. God wants to help you receive the blessing of a partner. Therefore, be willing to rest in the finished work of Jesus and benefit from God's wisdom and guidance.

If you commit to the process of growth, spiritual maturity, and change, then God's promise of a husband will unfold in your life at the right time. The fact is that you will get what God promised you. However, you must be willing to let God prepare you for the promise. Consider this following example to further understand the purpose and importance of the preparation period in your life. Imagine how ill-equipped one would be, if upon receiving the news of being pregnant, one didn't adequately prepare and make the required personal changes gradually over time, in anticipation of the day when the promised baby would be delivered. In fact, recognize it is best to make preparations and changes, which include living a healthier lifestyle, prior to becoming pregnant, in order to enhance the possibility of becoming pregnant and of having a healthy pregnancy and a healthy stable environment needed for the baby to grow and thrive.

This means you must make a full commitment to making changes, investing your full self in the process, and staying the course over time. You will benefit and get the fullest reward if you do. Take the opportunity, in this stretching and growing process, to lean completely on God. Also, focus on fostering a rich connection and relationship with your Abba Father, God, and Jesus. You will survive this process with their love, grace, compassion, strength, support, wisdom, and guidance. While praying and hoping for the blessing of a husband, also acknowledge the benefit of having the opportunity to develop a stable and stronger connection and relationship with God. You will be blessed trifold! Through it all, remember, you will receive the promise.

Today's Powerful Thought
I am willing to learn, grow, and mature in preparation for receiving the promise from God. I will be blessed.

Prayer
Abba Father, I ask You to walk with me and guide me through the growth, maturity, and changes I must make to develop, heal, and establish better relationships. Through it all, help me to remember that You are gently guiding me along the path that leads to a richer and more fulfilling life. Help me to endure and not to hide or shrink from the challenges I face as I take this journey. Help me to rely and depend on You to offer me love, support, kindness, compassion, security, safety, protection, peace, joy, and wisdom. Help me to draw from Your love to sustain me for the rest of my life. Help me to navigate the areas of growth, maturity, and change I need to engage in. Please help me to stay the course by Your grace. Help me to more fully walk in my righteous identity, which I have received

from Jesus. Thank You, Abba, for responding to my every need. Thank You that I will benefit from Your guidance and preparing. Thank You that I will receive the promise of a loving, positive, lasting relationship with a mate. In the name of Jesus, I pray. Amen.

DAY 18

DEALING WITH BREAKUPS

As you move forward and step out in faith to grow and experience God's love, is there something standing in your way of fully embracing love? Could it be that you are possibly impacted by a breakup with someone who deeply wounded your heart and impacted how you feel about yourself? Could it be that you have not let him go? What is it costing you to hold on to your past? You may not be receiving the husband you are patiently waiting for because you have not let go of somebody you once loved or perhaps still love very much.

Perhaps you are not satisfied with the lack of closure, or you may simply not feel like anyone else can measure up to this special person who got away. Perhaps the wounds were so deep that you are still hurt. You may even be afraid to try at love again or may not believe that anyone else can love you. Likely, you will never be truly able to move forward until you let go of your past. The questions you may be asking now are, "But how do I get over someone I can't seem to get over? How do I let go of my past, the pain I experienced, and the hopes I once had?" This is where many people stay stuck.

The simple truth is you do not need to remain hurt, afraid, angry, and resentful over what happened. You do not have to judge yourself by the quality of how you were treated by another person. God is already doing a new thing in your life. Accept with confidence that if someone walked away from a relationship with you, then God never intended it to last. His blessing is in a different place. It means that while you may be still focused on history, God has arranged blessings for you to receive in a relationship with an incredibly special person whom He chose. That person you may be holding on to from your past was never God's choice for you. You may be crying over someone who was never meant to be your special someone. It was always going to fail. Although it is difficult, you must let go of your past so you can receive someone who will enrich your life far greater than you ever dreamed or hoped possible.

Your past is a deceiver, which manipulates your sense of worth, identity, and hope for a better life. Someone in your past may have wounded you, hurt your pride, and rejected you, which made you believe you have no value and nothing of quality to offer. You may have struggled with not feeling good enough or even worthy of receiving respect, compassion, appreciation, kindness, validation, acknowledgment, acceptance, and love. You may have been so hurt and disappointed that you lost hope for a better future with someone else. Your diminished sense of self-worth and value may cause you to experience yourself as broken, bad, and abnormal. Eventually, an accompanying sense of deep-seated shame and humiliation may likely develop. You may struggle to respect and love yourself. You may experience yourself as being less worthy of respect, love, attention, caring concern, and a loving relationship. You may think you lack anything of value to offer another person and may fail to recognize how gifted, special, and really beautiful you are. On comparing yourself to others, you may feel inferior or of lesser quality. You may feel hopeless, lost, ashamed, empty, and unlovable. Ultimately, you may struggle with not having a stable and healthy identity.

The lesson comes through learning that your value, worth, respect, identity, and hope can never be derived from another human being. This is an important, although painful, lesson to learn. It acknowledges that who you are can never be defined and based on another person's treatment and evaluation of you, or the capacity of that person to love you in the quality way you deserve to be loved. These things must be received and experienced in your relationship with God and your connection with His Son, Jesus. Your worth, identity, and nature are entirely based on your relationship with God and Jesus. It is God's love that heals and gives you a sense of worth, value, and being good enough to be loved. Your relationship with Jesus gives you a sense of value and worth through the righteousness you have received from Him. From Jesus you have received a righteous identity and the identity of being a child of God and one in Spirit with Jesus (1 Corinthians 6:17, 2 Corinthians 5:21, Romans 8:9, 2 Corinthians 6:18, Galatians 3:26).

This acknowledgment releases any person who hurt you from ever needing to validate you or provide you with a sense of feeling lovable, good enough, worthy, special, and valuable. What someone did to you, or failed to do, cannot alter the worth, value, and quality of who you are. You have received an uncompromised worth, value, and identity from Christ Jesus, your Savior. It is a gift by grace and neither you nor another person can do anything to compromise who you are in Christ. Your worth, value, and identity are based entirely on Jesus and His worth, value, identity, and performance. Further, God loves and acknowledges you as His own child. He sees you as one with His Son, Jesus. He invites you to experience a loving personal relationship with Him.

This brings you to the most powerful way to receive healing from a broken heart and a past relationship that keeps you stuck. The answer lies in prioritizing your relationship with God as the most important relationship in your life. Yes, this is your powerful answer. This is the powerful solution, which will never compromise or diminish your value and worth. When you are in the presence of God and in a relationship with Him, you will experience love and compassion. You will experience perfect love, with such warmth and a sense of comforting peace like you have never experienced before. This is the only love capable of making you feel unconditionally loved, accepted, fulfilled, and complete.

After experiencing God's consistent, perfect love, over time the quality of His love will cancel all the detrimental effects of your past, negative relationships and deep pain. You will no longer feel undesirable, unworthy, and unlovable. Instead, you will have the positive experience of feeling wanted, cared for, appreciated, valued, and deeply loved. Your experience of God's love frees you from having to earn love or perform to win it. You experience feeling loved and accepted just as you are, even with your imperfections. As a direct result, your sense of personal value, worth, respect, and integrity are restored, but on a level that by far supersedes what existed before you experienced a personal connection and relationship with God.

God always welcomes you with an open heart. Never feel like you messed up too much or that you don't qualify or deserve to be in His presence. Never stay away because you feel distance. Even if your emotions make you feel separated or as if God has withdrawn His presence, you can always go to Him. He is never truly distant or far away. He is always close. He will never turn you away. You are important to Him. He offers the love you have been seeking. God promised you that neither death nor life, nor angles nor principalities, nor powers, nor things present nor the future and things to come, nor height, nor depth, nor any other created thing would ever be capable of separating you from His love, which is in Christ Jesus (Romans 8:38–39). He loves you so much that He paid the ultimate price to save you when He paid with the sacrifice of His beloved Son Jesus (John 3:16).

He did this so that we could be called daughters and sons of God (1 John 3:1). He loves you and wants to establish a relationship with you so that you will benefit, be protected, prosper, and experience His love, which heals you in every area of your life. You never have to compromise to be perfectly loved by God.

How else can you get over that person from your past? Focus your thoughts, beliefs, feelings, and behaviors on spiritual words, which anchor you in faith and God's love for you. Make meditating on God's Word a priority in your life. Ask God to lead you to scripture which offers you comfort, wise counsel, and helps you heal from the pain of a broken heart. It is beautiful when you let God's Spirit guide you and help you. Actively engage in fellowship, worship, and study when seeking spiritual edification and God's guidance. Seek spiritual edification and counsel from a person who is mature in his or her walk of faith. God's Spirit will guide you to the right person. You need never walk your journey alone.

In forming a deeper and closer relationship with God, make time to also give Him praise. You will find that the benefits to you are tremendous! Praise may be done in so many beautiful ways. You will discover that listening to music, singing, and praying with a focus on praise to God uplifts your spirit and provides relief from burdens. Further, you more powerfully experience God's loving and compassionate presence, as well as His strength and peace. You no longer feel alone and sad. In those moments of praise, you discover relief from your fears, anxieties, worries, pain, and hopelessness. You feel encouraged and are reassured that God provides what you need. Moments of praise bear witness to God's majesty, power, and control over every situation or circumstance. You realize you are under His care and protection, that He is greater than anything you face, and that He fights your battles for you. Give praise for His blessings and for providing for you.

Don't be disappointed in what didn't work out or who walked away. The breakup was God's will. If you hold on to what God wants you to let go of, then you will block your own destiny and the loving relationship God wants you to enjoy with someone new. Move forward toward the wonderful life and future God has planned and provided for you. Pray to have a new relationship, according to His will, purpose, and plan for your life and to His glory.

Today's Powerful Thought

I can let go of my past and get over my breakup by enjoying a beautiful relationship with God who loves me more deeply than anyone else. He has a beautiful future planned for me.

Prayer

Thank You, Abba Father, for protecting me from a relationship that I wanted but would have been bad for me and hurt me even more deeply. Please help me to let go of my past and move forward into the destiny You have planned for me. Thank You that I can rely on Your love, understanding, and warmth to help me heal. I know You have the best planned for me and that one day I will have a new relationship with someone I love, who loves me as You wish for us to love each other. Thank You that my pride does not have to be wounded and that Your love heals me. Thank You that my worth and value are not derived from others but comes from You and through Jesus. Thank You for Your love, grace, favor, protection, and forgiveness. Thank You that in You, Abba, I have hope for a new love and life. In the name of Jesus, I pray. Amen.

DAY 19

PRAYING IN FAITH TO MOVE FORWARD

With God's love, you can go forward. You have got to try again! This time, however, benefit from receiving His wisdom and by following His will. Cooperate with God and work as a team, operating under His authority, will, and guidance. Your experiences have taught you the invaluable lesson that doing things your own way does not lead to the results you want. It is very debilitating to suffer from a broken heart and disappointed hopes due to the painful loss of love and rejection. It may make you want to give up on love entirely, burying your hopes and dreams. You may also bury your heart and, with it, barricade yourself from love, because you fear being even more deeply hurt by another disappointment in love.

Being vulnerable in love and opening your heart to love again does not often feel good or even safe when your heart has been broken and you are still hurting. However, I encourage you to not give up on love, because no weapon formed against you will prosper (Isaiah 54:17). This includes the weapons of grief, loss, and the profound sadness you experience due to having a broken heart.

It may be difficult to move forward in love when sadness overwhelms you. You may not even realize it, but buried deep within your heart, unconsciously, you may feel like when he walked away, he also took your hope of having a future where you are loved and happy in a good relationship with a partner. As a result, you may experience grief, hopelessness, and a crippling loss of dignity and personal value. This impacts every area of your life, including your ability to function and maintain a positive stable mood and sense of self. You may find yourself challenged in interacting with others, where you wrestle with not feeling good enough or worthy of their love, attention, time, respect, caring concern, and valuing of you as a person. You may also struggle with feeling disposable and unimportant to others.

To counteract these feelings and as a way to maintain connection and relationship, you may assume the role of the helper, who tries to be useful by fulfilling the wishes, needs, and desires of others, even if it means putting yourself last and not having others reciprocate. Recognize, this also comes from a desire to earn value based on what you do for others, thereby demonstrating that you may be of value to others. The hope of course is that you will be loved. It is not uncommon to feel trapped in this cycle of emotional and interpersonal patterns, which ultimately only make things worse and are difficult to alter. Over time, you may find yourself unable to sustain positive emotions and may frequently feel overwhelmed by intensely felt negative emotions.

However, no matter what you are experiencing or challenged with, God's promises to you are real and not dependent on your emotions, how other people treated you, your current circumstances, or what happened in your past. God's plans are to bless you and give you hope and a future (Jeremiah 29:11). This promise means that He will heal you from pain and overwhelming emotions and guide you to a better place and a brighter future. His promise means that He will do most of the work. He will put the blessed plans for your life in place and influence the outcome in your favor. He will bring it to pass. No matter what happened in the past, you can place your hope in God's promise of blessings and a future that is better than you dreamed of. This is good news indeed!

Your past does not define the rest of your life. Trust God at His Word. God cannot lie (Numbers 23:19). You can expect to be blessed. His plans are to bless you and give you a good future, no matter what happened in your past or who walked away and hurt you. You do not have to give up on love or live in fear of hurt and disappointment. God has what you need. Remember, He is the God who supplies all your needs (Philippians 4:19).

This is your fresh start. Rest and trust in God. He offers you His reassurance in His Word to comfort and prepare you. Isaiah (43:18–19) says, "Do not remember the former things or consider the things of old. I am about to do a new thing, now it springs forth. Do you not perceive it? I will make a way in the wilderness and rivers in the desert." What this means is that this is the springtime of your new life. With God, there is no limitation of time, age, or distance. He has no limitation at all.

Focus on the fact that God is **El Shaddai**, God Almighty, the all-powerful, all-sufficient one (*Hebrew translation of one of the names of God, see notes section*[1]). He is the God of all creation and the entire universe. He is perfect, omnipotent, and completely sufficient in all (for example—love, grace, blessings, provision, and protection). How is it that you fear and doubt? It is God who will accomplish it on your behalf. You need only trust in Him and walk step by step with Him as He guides you and makes the way clear.

So be encouraged and go to God in prayer. Talk to Him. You can pour out your heart to Him without shame or fear. He is always available and welcomes you. He is waiting to receive you and offer you His loving, peaceful, reassuring, and comforting presence, as well as His compassionate, listening heart. Although at times it may be difficult to manage your own feelings, in the presence of God you will no longer feel so overwhelmed. You can give your cares and concerns to Him. He takes your burdens and provides the strong shoulders you need to lean on. Try it and you will experience how God works on your behalf. Let God's love, presence, and power heal you and work on your behalf to bless you and give you hope and a good future.

Focus on being a loved, righteous child of God through Christ (2 Corinthians 5:21, Galatians 3:26). Remember that you are a new creation in Christ and that old things have passed away and no longer have power over you (2 Corinthians 5:17). By His (Christ Jesus) stripes, you are healed (Isaiah 53:5). Therefore, by His stripes you are healed from a broken heart, anxiety, fear, shame, disappointment, sadness, grief, hopelessness, despair, and the effects of the past. The precious body and blood of Jesus qualify you for healing, joy, a loving relationship, and a blessed life of favor. It is all yours to receive by the grace of God and the finished work of Jesus on the cross.

Today's Powerful Thought

I am assured that because God loves me and Jesus' blood was shed for me, I am healed from the past, a broken heart, and overwhelming negative emotions, and move forward to experience a loving relationship with someone else.

Prayer

Abba, please heal my broken and hurting heart today. Help me to feel Your love and Jesus' love for me. I know that by the sacrifice of Jesus for me, I am healed of this sadness, despair, shame, disappointment, regret, resentment, anxiety, fear, loneliness, grief, and hopelessness. Please help me to feel Your comforting and compassionate presence in this moment. Help me to love again and be open to loving others. Thank You, Abba, that I can move forward to enjoy the blessings, and life of hope and prosperity that You have promised and planned for me. In the name of Jesus, I pray. Amen.

DAY 20

GOD IS LOVE

Sometimes, it can be difficult to believe that God has a better life for you to receive when you are in distress or not feeling able to function at full capacity. You may feel overwhelmed when things do not quite work out how you expected, or the journey becomes difficult to endure. In these moments, you may wonder if God will truly ever bless you or respond to your needs. However, in the midst of fears, doubts, disappointments, sadness, despair, anxieties, and not feeling like you can endure, God urges you to focus your attention on Him and who He is. He asks you to trust Him and believe in His Word and promises for your life. However, it may be a struggle to do this if you do not know God's true nature and character.

You may ask, "How can I know with certainty who God really is?" To know who He is, you can invite the mystery of God to unfold by investigating the scriptures for the truth about God's real nature, character, and identity. By reading His Word, you will begin to know Him. You can also invite the experience of being in His presence and developing a closer and more personal relationship with Him over time.

In His Word, we learn about one of the most wonderful qualities of God's nature. God is love (1 John 4:7-19). God's nature is love. He is revealed as the source and supply of love itself, for as 1 John 4:7 tells us, love is from God. This means that God is the source and originator of love. Being the source and originator, His love is perfect and complete love. Therefore, what God offers you is love in the best form. It is perfect, unconditional love, which never fails to fully satisfy you. There is also no fear or punishment in His love for you (1 John 4:18). This means you never need to fear God or expect punishment from Him. You never have to fear harsh treatment, judgment, condemnation, and rejection. God loves you with perfect, loving kindness forever, which is not based on your performance or how much you love Him or deserve His love (1 John 4:10). What this means is that you never have to qualify for God's love. His love is freely offered, and nothing makes Him withhold it from you. Knowing this, you can experience peace.

The true character of God's love is also revealed in the sacrifice of His Son Jesus for you. God sacrificed His own beloved Son Jesus and offered Him in your place because He loves you (John 3:16-17). He loves you so much that He did not want to be separated from you or allow you to be punished and condemned to death. He offered Jesus as the atoning sacrifice for your sins so you might be saved and live through His Son (1 John 4:9-10). Jesus received your punishment and condemnation so you would be saved. He paid the price for you, suffered in your place, and took your punishment. God offered Him because He so loved you (John 3:16). He loves you so much, He did not withhold even His own beloved Son. What is also important to realize is that

God and Jesus are one (John 10:30, John 1:1-2). What does this mean? God loves you so much that He gave of Himself to save you.

What more do we know about the true nature of God's love? In Corinthians 13, the nature of love is described in more detail. We are told that love is patient, kind, not irritable or angry, not envious, not boastful, not rude or disrespectful, and not selfish. It is honest, tells the truth, does not hide, and endures (interpreted to mean forever, no matter the circumstances or how you behave or fail to perform). God loves you perfectly, which means that He demonstrates these qualities of love perfectly and consistently. His love lacks nothing. He never fails at loving you. The truth is, His love patiently perseveres and is everlasting, over the course of your life, as you go through various hardships and problems.

The love that Jesus demonstrated toward others when He was on Earth further reveals the nature and quality of God's love for you. Several scriptures reveal how Jesus was often moved with deepest loving compassion for others and, as a result, relieved the suffering of others and healed them (Matthew 9:36, Luke 7:12-15, Matthew 14:14, Matthew 20:34, Mark 8:2-3). Jesus also demonstrated compassionate forgiveness, even when He was on the cross being crucified for man's sins (Luke 23:32-43). He did not consider His own suffering but rather, was moved by love to feel compassion, empathize with, understand, and forgive. Therefore, through Him, God's love is proven to be full of compassion, kindness, empathy, understanding, forgiveness, acceptance, and selflessness toward you today.

These characteristics of God's love are further demonstrated by how Jesus Himself demonstrated that He (Jesus) is the good shepherd who cares for, provides, protects, guides, and has conquered the world so that you will be okay and never have to pay the price for sin (Psalm 23, John 10:7, John 16:33). Jesus allowed Himself to be sacrificed and laid down His life for you. This demonstrates how loved, valued and important you are to God. It also shows how loving and unselfish Jesus was—by allowing Himself to be a substitute for you on the cross. In these actions, God is revealed to be a merciful, caring, unselfish, and self-sacrificing protector, who loves you very much.

God also proved that He would provide whatever is needed, by providing His own beloved Son as the sacrifice, without you having to suffer or offer anything yourself. This may be difficult to comprehend. However, it is no less true that God loves you so much that He withheld nothing, not even His own Son to save you (Romans 8:32). By offering Jesus as the sacrifice, He offered His very best to save you. His love offers the best quality. What is also revealed is that God's love never hides, but is always demonstrated, no matter the difficulties, obstacles, challenges, and problems that you face.

Therefore, you can experience His peace, knowing with confident faith that who God loves, He also provides for and protects (Psalm 127:2, 1 Timothy 6:17, Psalm 23, Psalm 91). Every good and perfect gift comes from the Father (James 1:17). What this means is that everything that is for your best, quality life is available right now by grace. You don't have to occupy yourself with wondering if your life will get better or with questioning if you've done enough or you are good enough. God offered His own Son as the sacrifice for you so that you could "freely" be given all things (Romans 8:32). His will is for you to be richly blessed, protected, and provided for. This includes having the blessing of a good husband and a loving relationship.

What this all demonstrates is another quality of the nature of God's love. His love is characterized by grace and mercy toward you (1 Timothy 1:12–15). This scripture confirms that no matter what you may have done or how lost you were in sin, Christ was sent into the world to save you. It says that by the grace and love that are in Christ, you benefit from not having to suffer for your sins. By love and grace, you are no longer dead in sins. God made Jesus, who knew no sin, to become sin for us all so in Him we might become the righteousness of God (2 Corinthians 5:21). Therefore, it is established that it is never about how good you are or how worthy you feel. You do not need to qualify to be loved. It is about how good Jesus is. Your sin debt has been cancelled based on Jesus' righteous sacrifice. It means that you are unequivocally free forever from the chains of sin.

You are no longer subject to punishment, condemnation, and death because of your sins. This means that He cancelled the power and negative consequences of sin in your life by giving you His righteousness and taking your sins into Himself to be punished in Him. Isaiah (53:5) says, "God is good and His mercies endure forever." He gave the offering of His Son and allowed Him to suffer in your place and pay the ultimate price for your sins. He also graciously allowed the transfer of His own righteousness to you, and had Jesus take your sins. Jesus took your sins and you received the righteousness of God through Him. Indeed, this is merciful, perfect love.

Jesus Himself also lets you know that God loves you just as much as He loves Him (John 17:23). Now take a moment and reflect on the quality and nature of God's love for Jesus. Jesus said God loves you equally. God loves you to an equal measure as He loves Christ the Lord. Permit yourself to connect with this truth. Further, through Jesus you are reconciled with God and have been accepted as a child of God (2 Corinthians 5:18-19, 2 Corinthians 6:18). In Christ you are a child of God through faith (Galatians 3:26). You are now an acknowledged, loved, and valued member of God's family forever. Do you know what else defines the nature of God's love for you? It can be summarized in this statement—Nothing can separate you from His love, that is in Christ Jesus your Lord (Romans 8:35-39).

Further, you are encouraged not to fear being in the presence of God and going to Him to receive His love, compassion, comfort, understanding, help, and protection. In the presence of God, you will absolutely encounter His loving nature and experience His perfect love. In His presence you will absolutely know with certainty that God is love. When you enter His presence, you will experience that His love is like a warm embrace. It provides shelter, protection, guidance, and a real sense of family, home, and belonging. In God's presence, you experience an intimate relationship between daughter/son and Father (Romans 8:15-16). He wants to be called Abba Father, which denotes His permanent designation as your loving Father, not a judge or someone to fear and be intimidated by. In Romans (8:15-16), you are encouraged not to fear God anymore, because the Spirit bears witness that He is your Abba Father and you are His child, whom He never judges or condemns. Further, you are asked to recall that you have been set free from the bondage and condemnation of the law. This is because Jesus paid the price for your sins and gave you righteousness so that you could now be free. You were made one with Him as a result and, through Him, became a child of God. Now you can say Abba Father with confidence and go to God to receive His love without fear.

You can be encouraged that because of God's perfect, complete, and merciful love, you are more than a conqueror (Romans 8:37). Therefore, you need never worry or fear about anything. His love and grace provide comfort and hope in every situation (2 Thessalonians 2:16–17). Further, you are told that God can be witnessed, known, and understood by the things He has made (Romans 1:20). Even if you only see God revealed just a little bit in the wonderful things and people He has made, what will become evident is His eternal, powerful, and divine nature (Romans 1:20). You will also witness the beautiful, loving nature of God and the care He took in making what you witness around you. Without any doubt, God is indeed love! He is your loving Abba Father, who will always respond to you with perfect love and help you in every situation.

Today's Powerful Thought
God is love.

Prayer
Thank You, Abba Father, that You are my Father who loves me perfectly and offers me Your grace,

mercy, forgiveness, compassion, understanding, acceptance, blessings, hopefulness, and help in every situation. Thank You for the loving sacrifice of Jesus in my place. Help me draw closer to receive Your never-ending supply of love right now. I know I am loved forever. In the name of Jesus, I pray. Amen.

DAY 21

GOD IS GENEROUS

When it comes to believing God for blessings in your life, it is important to reflect on what you know about who God is and what you can expect from Him based on His Word. We have already reflected on God's love for you in the previous chapter. His very nature is perfect love. Being loving and generous in nature, He gave His very own Son to save you. What an extraordinary gift He gave you by making Jesus, His own Son, your substitute, so that you would not be punished for your sins! This is why you can trust the Word when it says that God will not withhold any good thing from you (Psalm 84:11). The price He paid to save you and me was very high and actually worth way more than the sin debt of the entire world.

What does this sacrifice of His Son to save us tell us about God and who He is? God is loving and generous. His loving, generous nature withholds nothing. He offers His very best without restraint. His loving, generous nature says that there is nothing that is too good for you to receive. The acknowledgment is that God, who did not spare His own Son but sacrificed Him to save you, will most certainly freely give you all things (Romans 8:32).

As this verse in Romans says more specifically, "He who did not spare His own Son but delivered Him up for us all, how shall He not with Him also freely give us all things?" What it clarifies is the depth and quality of God's loving generosity. God will not hold back anything that is for your good and blessing.

Of course, He will answer your prayers and come to your aid. God will always offer His very best for your benefit. He willingly and freely gave up His own Son so that you would receive life and be set free from condemnation, punishment, and death. He gave beyond what was even required, in that Jesus is righteous and so perfect and divine, without sin or fault. Jesus is the Son of God and is one with God (John 10:30). God, the Father, is in Him (John 17:21). Therefore, you see why Jesus was far more valuable and outweighed Adam's sin and the collective sins of the world. God gave more than what was required as your solution. Therefore, you can trust that He will always absolutely generously give you all things, even beyond what you ever hoped for or expected.

God's generosity extended way beyond this. You have received the righteousness of God, in Christ, and have been made one with Christ in the Spirit (2 Corinthians 5:21, 1 Corinthians 6:17). You were given the righteousness of God and are one with Christ. In exchange, Christ took your sins. Most generous God, by doing this, made you one with Him, whereby the Father is now also in us. What an extraordinary gift! You are now, therefore, one with Jesus and God (John 17:20–23). To top it all, you have received the relationship and title of child of God (Galatians 3:26). You are reconciled to God as a child of God, who has received God's righteousness and glory through Christ Jesus (2 Corinthians 5:18, John 17:22). You are now a part of God's family.

Therefore, what can you know with certainty about God's generosity? Every good and perfect gift comes from the Father and is your blessing to receive today (James 1:17). Thus, you can trust God to generously bless you. He is beyond your human comprehension of generosity. He will provide for you. He will not withhold the blessing, especially now that you are His family. Therefore, have confident faith that you will receive the blessing of a good husband and every blessing God generously provides to His children.

Today's Powerful Thought
God is generous and generously gives
all things to me, His child.

Prayer
Abba Father, thank You for being so generous with me. When I needed a Savior, You sacrificed Jesus for me. Thank You that You give me every good and perfect gift, provide for me, and withhold nothing for my benefit and good, to Your glory, God. Generous Father, thank You that I am one with You and Jesus. Please grant me the desires of my heart to Your glory and help me to be faithful. I know I can trust You, Father. In the name of Jesus, I pray. Amen.

DAY 22

FAITH = 100 PERCENT GUARANTEED

When you examine your faith life in believing for something so big and exceptional like a husband, you may fail to see what is undermining your faith. One of the biggest ways your faith may be challenged is when you engage in the practice of constantly questioning God, including even after He offers you clarity. You may engage in habitually questioning even in the most seemingly benign ways. For example, you may ask, "God, I don't know how this is possible, will you please show me? Will you reveal it all to me instead of me going step by step not knowing? How can this happen now after everything? Is it still your will for me? I am scare that I may not see all I need to and something bad will happen, what should I do? Am I doing the right thing? Should I keep waiting or should I do something? I feel so confused. What is your plan for me? I feel like I am doing something wrong or not understanding you clearly. Please tell me what you want me to do? Could you please clarify or show me definitive proof or a sign of what you want me to do?"

Pay attention to every form of questioning God that you engage in. Buried behind each question are emotions of fear, anxiety, and worry, accompanied by doubt. These are the foxholes of faith, which sabotage your belief, trust, and confidence in God. They also interfere with experiencing His presence and peace, and block you from receiving His guidance and His leading by the Holy Spirit. It is difficult to accurately hear God when your emotions interfere with His peaceful presence and your faith.

When you examine what drives your habitual questioning, you will realize that it results from not trusting God and doubting that you can believe His Word or take Him at His word. You may discount yourself from having the right to expect that His Word applies to you or in your situation. You may feel disqualified or undeserving and fear that God does not care enough to protect, provide, or safeguard you. When you don't see the way clearly, you may find yourself drawing back, doubting your beliefs, and questioning God even more, which signal a hesitation to step out in faith and to trust and follow His plan and timing.

Sometimes, the questions come from believing you have not been good enough or performed to God's standards, and so you have cancelled your blessings and fallen out of favor or from grace being applied to you. You may fear condemnation and punishment. The truth is that the irrevocable blessings, favors, and calling of God are independent of your performance. You are righteous and blessed, based on Jesus and God's love, mercy, and grace.

How do you maintain faith? Simply have faith in God (Mark 11:22–24). This scripture alludes to you simply trusting God, with the simple, unquestioning faith of a child who knows she has a good, loving, and trustworthy Father, who has already proven Himself trustworthy. How did God prove Himself? The sacrifice of His own Son, Jesus, for you was the ultimate proof of His trustworthiness and perfect love for you (John 3:16–18). That is how you know you can have faith in God.

It also means knowing that God will not lie and, therefore, you can believe what He says in His Word and what He has promised you. Numbers 23:19 says that God is not a man that He should lie, and assures you that whatever He says He will do, He will do it. Therefore, you can absolutely take God at His word, even if you don't understand it all. It is promised that your belief, hope, and faith in God will never be put to shame or disgraced (Romans 10:11, Isaiah 54:4–5, Psalm 25:3). Faith knows that you can always trust God. Therefore, belief and trust in God are part of the core foundation of your faith.

Believing God and trusting Him will help you to have full conviction and faith. Jesus said that when you pray with this kind of conviction and believe that you have received whatever you prayed for, it will be yours (Mark 11:24). If you do not doubt in your heart, but have the full conviction of belief that it will happen, it will happen. You are instructed to pray for what you desire and to thereafter believe that you have received what you desired. This means that you accept in hope and faith, based on the irrefutable Word of God that God Himself will make it happen. The words "have received" also allude to the fact that it has already happened. This means that in the spiritual sense it is finished, and one hundred percent guaranteed.

Therefore, it is only a matter of time before it manifests in your life or the natural, physical plane of reality. It means that God orchestrates it into being in the natural. Once you pray, you do not have to keep questioning God or asking for proof and confirmation or looking for evidence that it will happen. Doing this undermines your restful state of convicted belief and faith in God and His Word, which are needed to bring what you prayed for into reality.

Instead of questioning, doubting, and being consumed by paralyzing, negative emotions, focus on words that build up your belief and faith in God, as well as confirm God's perfectly loving, compassionate, merciful, forgiving, generous, and protective nature. Jesus also instructed that the words you speak based on faith are powerful in activating your blessings and what you pray for. He said that if you speak with faith and do not doubt in your heart, but believe it will happen, then it will happen (Mark 11:23). The relationship between faith and the spoken word has another powerful connection. Faith comes by hearing the Word of God (Romans 10:17). Therefore, the words you speak yourself, and as a result also hear, have the power to enhance and strengthen your faith.

This suggests that you purposefully base your spoken words on the written Word of God, which reflects God's love, grace, power, promises, provision, protection, blessings, favor, and hope. Focus on aligning your spoken words with the written Word of God that addresses whatever situation, problem, or condition you are experiencing. Instead of asking questions or engaging in worry, fear, doubt, and despair, activate and enhance your faith by aligning your spoken word with the written Word of God. Do not speak words of doubt, fear, anxiety, sadness, despair, defeat, and hopelessness. Confess that the thing you prayed for will happen, according to God's will and purpose. Make statements based on the Word of God, according to His will and purpose, and to the glory of God, and do not doubt in your heart.

Praise God. Yes, also thank God with an attitude of joy, gratitude, and hopeful expectation. As Hebrews 11:3 says, "Call into being those things that not yet are as if they are." This is the way that God made the world. God's spoken words caused things to come into being, demonstrating the power of faith-filled, spoken words (Genesis 1:3–25). Also, Jesus performed many miracles by the words He spoke, for example, when He raised Lazarus from the dead (John 11:40–44). On this occasion, Jesus also thanked God and acknowledged that He knew God heard Him, even before He commanded Lazarus to come out of the tomb. Jesus, by doing this, demonstrated how we ourselves can apply spoken words of faith, an attitude of gratitude, and faithful belief in God when facing difficulties or praying for something.

Therefore, confess and speak in faith. Say, "Praise God I have it already. It is done through the finished work of Jesus on the cross." Believe in your heart and confess with your mouth, as you are instructed to do (Romans 10:8–10). This suggests the need to take an active role in bringing your faith and belief in God and Jesus into operation by speaking what you believe. It will not happen passively or by questioning God and trying to figure it all out on your own.

Instead, when you ask God for what you want, also ask that it be according to His will and to His glory. Then open your mouth to praise God and thank Him for hearing you and doing it for you, according to His will. Praise the glory of God. Make a command by faith, in the name of Jesus, knowing that in Him you have obtained grace, an inheritance, and hope (Ephesians 1:7–12). God's love and mercy provided that in Jesus, and through His sacrifice on the cross, all things are accomplished for you. Also, make your words a testimony to God's love, grace, blessings, protection, provision, promises, glory, power, and goodness. Let your words speak faith into your situation and reflect what you believe.

Something else you can do to operate in one hundred percent conviction and belief is to take steps forward as God directs you to, by faith. Believing and having faith before the promise takes place also mean allowing God to place you in the right position at the right time. It also means permitting God to direct you in making the needed preparations before the promise is fulfilled. Instead of being immobilized with anxiety and doubt, take the necessary steps to prepare for when the door to your promise is finally opened. Step out in one hundred percent guaranteed faith and make the changes and preparations needed to be prepared for what you have hoped for, to the glory of God and according to His will and purpose.

Stop questioning God. God's promises are one hundred percent guaranteed. No one who believes and places hope in Him will ever be put to shame.

Today's Powerful Thought
I trust God, and my faith in Him will never be put to shame. I will speak words of faith instead of doubts and fears.

Prayer
I know, Father, that You love me and that I can trust You. Please help me to stand in faith to experience a

life which is filled with many blessings, to Your glory. Father, let it all be accomplished according to Your will, plan, purpose, and timing, and not my own. I know I can trust You every time I recall how You offered Jesus as a sacrifice in my place. I confess that by faith I will receive all the beautiful promises You have made, Father, to Your children. I place my hopes for a good future in You, Father, and the blood of Jesus. Please show me what changes and preparations I need to make as I step out in faith and trust You to lead the way and prepare the path before me. Thank You for the opportunity and the blessings. By faith I believe. Help me to focus my thoughts and words on Your written Word. Please help me to feel Your love and provide me with the benefit of Your presence and wisdom. I love You, Abba, and I am so grateful for what I am about to receive, by Your love and grace. In the name of Jesus, I pray. Amen.

DAY 23

BLACK HOLES EXIST

Since the day you became a human being, unfortunately, you were never whole. This may be difficult to hear and contrary to everything you ever perceived about yourself, but no less true. Before we are reconciled with God, each one of us has a hole inside. The hole exists because we are cut off from a relationship with Jesus and God. This hole is most often experienced as a deep emptiness, void, and sense of isolation. Until the day you come into relationship with God and are born again through Christ and one with Him, you will always have a need and desire for someone or something to fill the hole.

Often, you may assume that other people who wounded you created the hole in you. The resulting experiences of hurt, inadequacy, unworthiness, guilt, shame, a sense of being unlovable, and negative emotions associated with the wound support the belief that someone else must be responsible for the hole.

While it is important to understand that, yes, what others did or failed to do did cause you tremendous pain and came with real negative consequences, this did not create the hole in you. These painful circumstances did not cause the hole and associated loss of sense of identity, self-worth and value, or accompanying emptiness, brokenness, fear, isolation, and despair. They were not the root cause of the hole in you. The pain others inflicted alerted you to the existence and presence of the hole. In other words, the hole always existed, but pain drew your attention to it and you became more consciously aware of it as a consequence of the pain you experienced due to the actions of others and other associated consequences that followed. It is like having a wound which you may not have full awareness of until you rub salt on it or it gets exposed to air, and then you become forcefully conscious of it and find it impossible to ignore. Neither the salt nor air caused the wound. They drew your attention and alerted you to the fact that you were deeply wounded, and appropriate intervention was therefore necessary, because your wound places you in danger.

When you have a hole and someone hurts you in an area associated with that wound or hole, such as by making you feel inadequate, unworthy, humiliated, disrespected, and unlovable, you will likely experience deep emotional pain. Depending on the situation and what you suffered, the impact may feel profound. For example, you may struggle to get past the pain or feel fearful, defenseless, and vulnerable. You may also feel stuck, helpless, angry, and incapacitated. Additionally, if you feel stuck in helplessness, anger, resentment, or emotional volatility, you may suffer from even more emotional pain. The hurt you experience in an area associated with the original hole or wound may make you desire someone to take care of you, love you, fix the wound, and make you feel whole again.

What you may now begin to understand is that you are responding as if someone caused your deepest wounds, which then formed a hole in you, when in reality, the hole in you already existed, and no person caused or created it. Your wounds and feelings of despair, fear, invalidation, unworthiness, unlovableness, emptiness, incompleteness, not being good enough, yearning, desire, need, loneliness, and a deep thirst for something more—in essence all your experiences associated with the hole in you—existed from the beginning of your life, here on Earth.

You may wonder where the hole came from. What caused it? The hole in you comes from being cut off from God due to Adam's original sin. Adam's sin resulted in mankind's loss of relationship with God. When he was separated from God, the wound was created in mankind. Adam's sin created the painful hole in you. It is a spiritual wound and, therefore, you require a spiritual solution for you to be healed and made whole. The obvious answer requires reconciliation and a relationship with God. It also requires that man no longer have a spirit characterized by the sin nature received due to Adam's original sin.

God provided the answer of how to fix the hole in the person of His own Son, Jesus. It is stated clearly in 1 Timothy 2:5-6. It states, "For there is one God; there is also one mediator between God and humankind, Christ Jesus, Himself human, who gave Himself a ransom for all; this was attested at the right time." In this, you are reassured that there is reconciliation between God and man, and a relationship with God, through His Son, Jesus.

When Jesus was crucified for you, He took your sin nature away and gave you His nature, which is the righteousness of God (2 Corinthians 5:21). You are no longer in the flesh but in the Spirit, having been made one with Christ Jesus and receiving the Spirit of God, which dwells in you (1 Corinthians 6:17, Romans

8:9–11). Therefore, you have been made a new creation in Christ, reconciled to God, and have become a child of God, through the sacrifice of Jesus for your sins and the sins of mankind (2 Corinthians 5:14–19, John 1:12). Once you believe, you no longer have to suffer being cut off from God, due to Adam's original sin. For by one man's (Adam) sin, condemnation and death came into the world, and by Jesus you received righteousness, life, and reconciliation as children of God (Romans 5:21).

The hole in you has always existed, no other person really inflicted the wound, and the hole can only be healed by reconciliation with God, through Jesus. Therefore, you no longer need to look to another person, other than Jesus for your solution. No human or human relationship, not even a relationship with a mate, can fill your emptiness, desire, need, and thirst for love. Only reconciliation and a relationship with God, through Jesus will fill the hole. Your real need is for Jesus and God, and there is no substitute for either. The space filler and the ways you try to occupy or distract yourself to fix the hole will all come up short. Fixating on needing others to satisfy you or to make up for the damage and pain they caused will never be sufficient to heal you. The hole existed before everything that happened to you and prior to anything you ever did or the ways you compromised yourself. Jesus is your answer.

Yes, Jesus is your hole filler! You will feel whole and complete in your connection with Jesus and God. You will also experience overflowing, perfect love, which restores, heals, and makes you whole. As Jesus Himself confirmed, the love you receive will be of the same measure and equal to the love that God bestows on Him, Jesus (John 17:23). Whatever wounds you experienced will be healed. The simple truth is that God's love and grace offer you the right solution. Now you have discovered the truth. If you have been born again and have received Christ, then you are free of the pain of your past and the hole in you. Acknowledge what you have received in Christ Jesus and connect with the love of God for your answer.

Today's Powerful Thought
Through my connection with Jesus, I am reconciled to God and the hole in me is healed forever.

Prayer
Abba Father, thank You for helping me heal from the deep hole in me, the wounds of the past, and the pain that I suffered. Thank You that in Jesus I am healed and made whole. Thank You for the gift of grace and forgiveness. Thank You for helping me to face this truth about the hole in me and how to receive healing. Please help me to forgive those who hurt me. Help me to let go of the past and holding others responsible for the hole in me. Please help me to let go of my humiliation, shame, anger, disappointment, and grief over my painful past and those who hurt me. In the name of Jesus, I pray. Amen.

DAY 24

JESUS IS MY HOLE FILLER

In praying for a husband and believing God for a life mate, it is necessary to understand that you will never find satisfaction in somebody else. Often, you may become fixated on praying for love and a mate. However, it is important to not busily try to get someone else to fill the hole, emptiness, and need in you, or heal your wounds. While it is natural and tempting to do this, you will only discover that not even your "most perfect human mate" can do that job sufficiently. The hole in you can never be filled by a husband or your relationship with any human being. Getting married to feel loved, worthy, valued, safe, secure, protected, fulfilled, satisfied, and complete, or to have a sense of identity and purpose, is 100 percent guaranteed to fail. You will only experience disappointment, if you expect to.

You will also sabotage a very beautiful relationship and connection with another by attempting to have it serve a function it was never meant to. If you require him to be more than he is capable of being and fulfilling in your life, the relationship will ultimately suffer, and you will both individually suffer and potentially inflict pain on each other. You will experience disappointment and may become angry and resentful if you require more than he can give you. You may also find that your mate or potential mate may experience feeling invalidated, and like a disappointment to you, or think you lack understanding, kindness, respect, love, and empathy. Additionally, your mate may become resentful and be deeply hurt because he feels unappreciated and inadequate when he constantly keeps coming up short in trying to satisfy you and fulfill your needs. You will likely also suffer from similar feelings. The potential to inflict pain on each other is significant when you use someone to satisfy a need.

Ultimately, the relationship may fail to overcome these many challenges. What is perhaps the greatest tragedy is that you may never find your mate, or you may let go of him because you wanted him to fulfill a role he was never meant to fulfill. Perhaps you may also fail to appreciate and graciously acknowledge one another and the many beautiful qualities you both possess and bring to the relationship. You may fail to recognize and appreciate the most rare and essential beauty of that special someone else and the relationship itself because he keeps coming up short at fulfilling a need he was always 100 percent guaranteed to fail at fulfilling.

Yet we cannot diminish the importance of love. You will feel empty and life itself in general will feel empty and meaningless if you do not have love (1 Corinthians 13:1–3). Reflect for a moment on the acknowledgment made in this scripture. Love is qualitatively so important that it surpasses spiritual gifts, powers of prophecy, deep understanding of all mysteries and knowledge, strong faith, and giving away all you possess. So how is love connected to filling the hole in you? In truth, as 1 Corinthians 13 suggests, love is the correct solution. You do need someone to love you, heal you, and make you whole again, or essentially fill the hole in you. However, as much as another human or your partner loves you, his love will never be able to satisfy you or fill the hole in you. We often look for the perfect human mate to make us feel whole, healed, good enough, capable, adequate, loved, desired, valued, worthy, whole, and complete. However, not even the most perfect human mate can ever achieve this. It is impossible.

This type of fulfillment can never come from a relationship with anyone else, except God, through your relationship with Christ Jesus. God has called you to be reconciled to Him and to become one with Him through His Son, Christ Jesus. It is not complicated. This is the only way that the hole in you will be healed and you will feel perfectly loved, valued, respected, accepted, understood, forgiven, cared for, empathized with, whole, and generally safe, protected, and secure. It cannot be achieved any other way. As you read in the previous chapter, your hole is derived from not being reconciled to God and in a relationship with Him. Your need is a spiritual need. Therefore, the hole in you needs a spiritual solution.

Jesus paid your penalty for sin and made this all possible. The sacrifice of His body and blood offer you grace and mercy. He became sin for you and through Him you receive the righteousness of God (2 Corinthians 5:21). Through His stripes and what He suffered in your place, you are offered healing and a new life (Isaiah 53:5). Once you believe, you receive His Spirit and become a new creation (1 Corinthians 6:17, 2 Corinthians 5:17). Sin, death, and the law no longer have dominion over you through Christ (Romans 6:14-23). Sin is no longer your master and you are now no longer under the law. You are under grace and an instrument of righteousness. You have been set free through Christ Jesus (Galatians 5:1, Romans 6:14-23).

You have a new identity and nature in Christ and are a beloved child of God, and part of the family of God forever (John 1:12, Galatians 3:26, 1 John 3:1-2). When you believe, you are then reconciled to God (2 Corinthians 5:18). Therefore, only Jesus can fill your hole and reconcile you to God. Once reconciled, it is your relationship with Jesus and God that offers healing.

The truth that must be acknowledged is that you need a spiritual solution to feel whole, healed, and loved. It is not wise to mistakenly believe that a mate is meant to complete you, make you feel whole, heal you, and satisfy your need to be loved. The belief—that you need to be joined with your complementary human mate to feel whole and that you will be incomplete without each other until you become one—is not accurate. The approach of trying to find the right person, your complementary half in another person, to complete you will never satisfy or fulfill your need to be loved or fill the hole in you.

Yet, your life may still feel less full until you have a partner to share your journey through life together. Recognize how God demonstrated this with Adam when He created Eve. Adam walked with God and—in his relationship with Him—had purpose, responsibility, power, connection with all living things on Earth, and a fully formed and completely whole identity and self. Yet God said it was not good for man to be alone, so God created a partner and helper for Adam (Genesis 2:18, Genesis 2:21-24). In this time, before Adam sinned, Adam had a close relationship with God but God acknowledged that Adam needed more for a fuller and richer life, to preserve, intact, the character of both of Adam's natures—his spiritual and physical forms. God withdrew Eve from Adam's side, as his helpmate and partner, to walk side by side through life with. When you are reconciled to God through Jesus and receive the gift of righteousness and healing through Him (Jesus), then you are made whole and complete. You experience the true, perfect love you have always been yearning. A human mate adds to the experience of a richer, quality life.

Your mate, however, does not have to be perfect or love you perfectly. Neither can either of you be a broken half of a person seeking to become whole and complete through marriage to a mate. God designed you to be complete and whole in Him through Jesus. He intended mates or partners to be two whole persons who complement one another and are designed to fit. It is intended that each of you be whole and complete through your important connection with Jesus, in whom you become righteous and reconciled to God, as His child. A mate cannot be a substitute for Jesus in your life. It is only through Jesus that you can become whole.

Marriage, therefore, is the union of two whole people who become one. Each partner must feel loved, experience being righteous, worthy, whole, and fulfilled spiritually through Christ Jesus. Each partner should have a core identity based on his or her connection to Jesus and relationship with God, versus the quality of the relationship with each other. Although your partner loves you, he will never be required to fill the hole in you, because he cannot.

Therefore, you see that God provided a beautiful means of preserving the character of both your natures—your spiritual form and your physical form. You will feel perfectly loved, whole, and fulfilled spiritually through Christ. At the same time, your desire to live a fuller life in human form may also be achieved through marriage, as you and your mate love each other, endure, persevere, grow, learn, and experience life's challenges and joys in your journey through life together. In your marriage relationship, you will then be free to function as two whole partners and helpmates who complement each other and are one with Christ.

Therefore, your marriage will also have Christ at the center and core, making for a stronger connection and spiritual bond between you and your mate over the course of your life together. Once Christ is at the center and core of your marriage, recognize that He is able to do what you cannot accomplish on your own. He offers wisdom and helps you through the challenges and storms you will inevitably face, making for a stable, stronger marriage that lasts over time. He also helps you to love each other as He loves you, with empathy, forgiveness, acceptance, and faithfulness, even when you each hurt the other or display faults and areas of needed growth and maturity.

Seek unconditional, perfect love, acceptance, comfort, peace, joy, healing, wholeness, and worthiness in a relationship with Jesus and God. Nothing else will ever satisfy you or provide you with what you need. There is no substitute for your relationship with Jesus. However, a beautiful marriage between your whole self and a whole mate, with Christ at the core, will add to the quality of your life.

Today's Powerful Thought
Jesus is my hole filler.

Prayer
Thank You, Abba Father, that You provided Your Son Jesus, who reconciled me to You. Thank You for Your perfect love, which I receive as Your child. Thank You for healing my wounds and making me feel worthy, whole, and complete. Thank You for the gift of righteousness, which I have received through Christ by grace. Jesus, merciful Savior, please draw near to me now so I may benefit from receiving Your loving, peaceful, healing presence and feel whole, in unity with my Abba Father. In the name of Jesus, I pray. Amen.

DAY 25

TEMPTATION

And Jesus being full of the Holy Ghost (Holy Spirit), returned from the Jordan and was led by the Spirit into the wilderness. Being forty days tempted by the devil. And in those days he did eat nothing: and when they were ended, he afterward hungered. And the devil said unto him, "If thou be the son of God, command this stone that it be made bread." And Jesus answered him, saying, "It is written, 'That man shall not live by bread alone, but by every word of God.'
—Luke 4:1–4

Jesus was hungry. When Satan urged Him to turn the stone into bread, Satan basically tempted Him to take a substitute (the stone), with the false promise that He could eat it and be satisfied. Recall, however, that Jesus is Himself the bread of life (John 6:33–35). We see in this temptation, Satan's attempt to activate lust and desire. When you are lonely and hungry and thirsty for love, Satan likewise activates thoughts of lust and desire. Once activated, Satan presents someone to occupy your lust and desire. You then try to fill your loneliness, hunger, and thirst for love with the person Satan offers to satisfy your need for love.

Satan tempts you to eat based on your lust and desire, not love. He will trick you into lusting and desiring what he presents, even if you do not truly love, value, respect, or want that person. Satan tempts you with lust and desire by telling you, "Someone special for you will never appear. Someone you value, respect and love could never love you. You cannot survive this loneliness, and nothing better is coming. You are not worthy; no one could ever love, respect, and value you, so you better settle for someone who is available, who shows interest in you, who needs you, or lusts and desires after you. This will fill your loneliness and hunger for love, at least until someone special comes along. Try it; this person could be someone special. Maybe you could make it work. It might be better than you expect. Try to fill your loneliness and hunger for love with this person so you won't hurt so much."

Satan offers to satisfy your need for love with what you will find is an experience that diminishes your sense of worth, value, integrity, and respect for yourself. You will enter a vortex of emotional turbulence and diminishing hope. Eventually, you may feel trapped and powerless to escape each time you give into Satan's temptation. Each time you partake of what Satan offers, your sense of worth, value, integrity, and self-respect will diminish even more, until it feels irretrievable. However, remember, God has already offered you the bread of life, His beloved Son, Jesus. Jesus gives you love, value, worth, righteousness, and establishes you as a beloved child of God, joint heir with Him, and one with Him in Spirit (2 Corinthians 5:18–21, Romans 8:15–17). Jesus is your hole filler.

Satan was attempting to draw Jesus out of recollection of who He is. Jesus is the Son of God and bread of life. Satan tempted Jesus to focus on His flesh and move out of His spiritual nature. He wanted Jesus to focus on His weakened and deprived temporary human condition and to believe this was His permanent state. He wanted Him to feel abandoned, alone, and desperate and to respond in a fleshly nature.

What Satan tried to do to Jesus is just what he tries to do to you. He tempts you by offering you what will never truly satisfy, but instead devalue your sense of worth, value, identity, and integrity. It will also attack your spiritual nature in Christ, and make you also feel condemned, alone, abandoned by God, and desperate. In fact, it draws you out of focusing on your spiritual nature and identity, and the grace and promises of God, and into focusing on your own limited human condition, power, strength, ability, and efforts. It also interferes with your connection with Jesus and God.

If you partake of what he offers, you find yourself in a worse condition, feeling disqualified from being in a relationship with Jesus and God, and from the benefits, blessings, and protections of being a child of God. Further, you feel even more alone and hungry for love and an emotional connection.

Satan tempts you by offering you flesh (satisfaction in lust and desire for someone else), when what you truly need is spiritual and cannot be satisfied by anyone other than Jesus and God. This is why you see that Jesus responded by saying, "Man shall not live by bread alone, but by every word of God." In this, Jesus confirmed what you should partake of in your need and hunger. To protect you and provide for you, you are instructed to focus on the written Word of God.

This means—be careful about the words you speak. Make sure you quote the written Word of God and speak this in the presence of your condition and situation. Make sure you speak words about God's love, grace, your righteous identity in Christ, and your position of being a beloved child of God. Also, pray, aligning your prayer with His Word. Pray with confident faith about His promises of blessings and protection for you. Thank Him for His promises being fulfilled, in faith. Pray about your situation and condition, knowing positively that you are loved and cared for. Read His Word. Meditate on scripture. Ask yourself, "What do I know about what God's Word says?" Quote His Word often in your common day, and especially when you feel weak, alone, unloved, weary, hopeless, tempted, stressed, and overwhelmed. Say, "It is written," just like Jesus did.

Draw love, strength, fulfillment, nourishment, identity, value, integrity, and respect from the Word of God. Draw these things from your spiritual relationship and connection with God and Jesus. Let your spoken words and thoughts reflect what the written Word says about these things, as they relate to you. Jesus is your bread of life. It is written that it is through Him (Jesus) that you can be confident that the promises of God are "Yes" and will be fulfilled (2 Corinthians 1:20). Therefore, you can confidently say "Amen," knowing it will all be accomplished through Jesus' finished work on the cross. You simply must believe.

You do not have to do it all alone or based on your own effort and ability. Do not be tempted to settle for less or to abandon your secure and blessed position of provision and protection as a righteous and beloved child of God, in Christ (2 Corinthians 5:18–21, Galatians 3:26). Have an expectation of good in your life by faith, even if you don't see it as yet (Hebrews 11:1). Do not be tempted to settle for less or to operate in lust, desire, need, and pride. God will fulfill it all for you.

Today's Powerful Thought
Jesus is my guarantee that God's blessings will be fulfilled in my life. I don't need to give in to settling for less!

Prayer
Thank You, Abba Father, that You love me. Thank You for Your grace toward me. I ask that You help me to not compromise or forget about Your love, mercy, and grace, which offer me provision and protection in all areas of my life and need to Your glory. Thank You that Jesus is the bread of life, and that all that I need is provided and accomplished through Jesus' finished work on the cross. Thank You that having a loving relationship is accomplished through Christ and Your grace. Help me to rest in Your peace, safety, and security, in the secret place of the Most High, knowing I am perfectly loved. Thank You for showing me how to not give into temptation by speaking Your written Word into every situation and condition I face. In the name of Jesus, it is accomplished. Amen.

DAY 26

SPIRIT OF LIFE NOT DEATH

Do not remember the former things, or consider the things of old. I am about to do a new thing, now it springs forth, do you not perceive it?
—Isaiah 43:18–19

In your season of grief and loss over past relationships, it is important to connect with your genuine feelings and allow yourself to mourn. Loss is considered a part of life. Likewise, mourning is also a naturally occurring process. It naturally helps you to heal from your broken heart, painful hurt, and disappointment you are likely feeling now. Just as important and, perhaps of even more value, is your willingness to mourn and let go.

Once a relationship is over, you must willingly accept the loss as well as accept that you are destined for something more. How do you know this? You have received God's promise that you will receive a new thing (Isaiah 43:18–19). He asks you to no longer look back at the past, but to let go of a dead thing. You must be willing to let go of the old thing before the new thing can be received. It is just that simple. A season of mourning signals a new, promised beginning.

If you compromise on letting go and instead hold on to the past, old relationships, and hurt out of a sense of loyalty, because you have invested so much of your time and self, or out of a sense of anxiety, fear, pride, jealousy, lust, desire, pity, sympathy, disappointment, sadness, self-sacrifice, hopelessness, guilt, self-condemnation, anxiety to be loved, envy, anger, or resentment, you will ultimately block your own path to happiness. You cannot expect to hold on to the past and bad or unhealthy relationships, and also reach your full potential and attain the fullest measure of blessings, provision, and protection from God. In this experience, you must recognize that it is God's will for you to let go.

Ultimately, you will suffer if you hold on to what God wants you to let go of. You must be willing to let go. This means no doors can remain cracked or partially opened. Letting go means closing doors. You must be willing to close the door and walk away forever. You will complicate your life and destroy any possibility of ever receiving a loving, beautiful relationship with who God provides the opportunity for you to love and experience love with if you don't let go completely, grieve your losses, and move forward. Looking back will compromise your future. Looking backwards is a path that leads to death, while the Spirit of life comes from your belief and faith that God offers you a better life, which He has already prepared for you to enjoy. The Word of God in Isaiah (43) confirms that indeed God wants to protect you and so offers you a new thing, which is already springing forth. Remember, in the middle of your grief, that the new thing, the new life that God provides is for your fulfillment, protection, and abundant provision.

But how do you know which doors to close? Let the Spirit of the Lord lead you, and in faith pray for wisdom, discernment, guidance, and strength. Ask God for confirmation and divine guidance from the Holy Spirit. Rest in God's peaceful presence and operate in faith, knowing that God has His best planned for you. If you rest and enjoy His peaceful presence, then this will guarantee that you experience the inner peace needed to hear God's Word and to be led by the Holy Spirit. This provides the opportunity for your spirit to commune in union with God, Jesus, and the Holy Spirit.

Your connection with God as His child through Christ guarantees that you are loved, provided for, and protected by grace (2 Corinthians 6:17-18, Galatians 3:26, Philippians 4:19). You don't have to qualify or strive by your own extraordinary efforts to attain the love, promises, and the provision of God. They are all yours by grace. In Isaiah (43:18-19) you see that God is making the promise that He will do it Himself. Therefore, know that God will guide you into His promise and make the path clear for you. Take it step by step with God, without fear, and trust His leading and direction. He will let you know which doors to close and provide peace in your spirit when you rest in His peace. Often, He will close the door Himself, but you must cooperate, walk away, and let the door remain shut.

Therefore, it is essential that you follow God's plan and will for your life, or else nothing will turn out as you expected or hoped for in your life, despite your best intentions and efforts. When God guides you, He will impart a sense of peace. In your spirit, you will experience His Spirit of peace. This helps you to receive His Word when you pray and to discern His leading by the Holy Spirit and His written Word in scripture. God will reveal His will and answers in His written Word and by His Spirit. His answers will make perfect sense for your life and guide you to the path that is best for you.

When you look at the closed doors in your life, you will recognize some common themes. Look and ask yourself, "What do I know about the things that transpired in my life? What patterns do I see? How was I impacted by my actions each time when I followed my own wisdom or sense of what was right? What are the common themes in my patterns of loving others or trying to attain and win another person's love? What are the common patterns and themes of those who loved me or who I thought loved me, but then hurt me?" Do you recognize the common themes and patterns? I assure you, they are there if you look closely enough.

Look and observe how many of your customary patterns and themes resulted in a life of pain, hurt, rejection, invalidation, failure, guilt, condemnation, despair, hopelessness, a diminished sense of feeling lovable, isolation, loneliness, and diminished self-worth and value. Do you see how they were contrary to God's Word, plan, and will? Do you see how the people, actions, and paths you chose were not God's best for you?

Closed doors and disappointments in life and love are often part of God's active protection of you. By closing doors in your life, God ensures that no harm will come to you. Closed doors and disappointments also ensure that you will not be tempted beyond what you can bear. They safeguard you and protect you from engaging in behaviors and actions that may turn out to be detrimental or not for your good. They guide your course, place you on the right path, and safeguard the destiny God has planned for you. Continuing on the course you were on may have harmed you and others more deeply, beyond what you or they suffered already or ever imagined possible.

Rather than staying stuck in holding on artificially, allow yourself to experience grief, knowing it will naturally dissipate over time, as you move forward in God's wisdom, to engage in the new life God has promised, full of good things (Isaiah 43:18–19). All you have to do is believe. Further, why continue to remain stuck in a protracted period of grief or painful emotions over someone or something that was meant for the harm of yourself and others? The door is best closed for your good and the good of others.

You also see that in Isaiah, God promises and reassures you that you will receive a quality life, better than before. He promises to do something new in your life (Isaiah 43:18–19). Recognize that all you simply have to do is rest, watch it spring forth, and enjoy the quality of what God produces for you to receive. He is purposefully setting you apart to receive His abundant supply of blessings. Yes, get ready for a new thing to spring forth and bloom in your life.

What I love most about this promise is that God Himself reassures that He will do it Himself. You don't have to be preoccupied with trying to make it all happen by yourself. The scripture says that God is about to do the new thing. It also says that already it springs forth, which means that it is already a present solution and new thing. God has ordained it so. All you have to do is witness it and enjoy and reap the benefits of God working on your behalf. He asks you to watch it unfold into reality in your life. You benefit without doing anything. This is exactly how

God's grace operates in your life. He sacrificed His own Son to save you, so that by grace, you can live a quality, rich life, the best life possible. You don't have to qualify to be blessed, and no one can take away God's blessings in your life. This scripture asks you to assume a posture of rest and confident expectation of good.

Remember that God, who did not spare His own Son Jesus, but sacrificed Him for us all, how would He not, with Him, also freely give us all things (Romans 8:32)? Yes, Christ Jesus is your bread of life, your Savior, and through Him, you are entitled to an abundant supply of blessings based on Jesus' righteousness, performance, and finished work on the cross, not your own. God blesses you freely and generously by grace because He loves you. He offered Jesus, His most valuable and very best offering, to save you, so know this means that He will freely offer you all good things and blessings. You are asked to look and discern how God is manifesting your blessings, new opportunities, and better relationships in your life. You simply must only accept Jesus as your Lord and Savior and believe in faith, then let God do the work on your behalf. What a blessing!

Often, when doors are closed by God, you will find yourself pushing against what seem to be the forces of nature, in the form of great difficulties and obstacles, which seem to place you in distress, wear you out completely, and deplete your resources. You may find yourself acting impulsively and desperately, with few quality returns on your costly, time-consuming, exhaustive efforts. When you find yourself fighting against what seems like a massive force of gravity, stop, consult God for guidance and wisdom, and rest in God's care. Then let His grace and love provide the path and orient you in the right direction. Let Him produce the planning, labor, and effort. You need only engage in the efforts He leads you to engage in. Believe and perceive your new thing unfolding. Draw even closer in relationship with God and Jesus, focusing on God's Word, grace, and love.

Do you know what else God's Word says? When God gives you something, it is good, and He blesses it. For you are reassured that "the blessing of the Lord makes rich and He adds no sorrow with it" (Proverbs 10:22). You can expect to be satisfied and not harmed by God's rich supply of blessings. Remember, God has promised to supply all of your needs according to the riches of His glory in Christ Jesus (Philippians 4:19). Therefore, when you rest and allow Him to take charge and bring a quality relationship into your life, you will not be harmed but, instead, richly blessed. It will all be accomplished by the grace that you have received through Christ.

Today's Powerful Thought
When I let go, the blessings of God unfold
in my life for my good, and I do not have
to work so hard to receive them.

Prayer
Thank You, Father, for bringing me into the secret
place of the Most High, with You and Jesus, where I
can rest and receive every blessing of protection and
provision to satisfy all of my needs. Please help me to
let go of my past and relationships that You want me

separated from. Help me to mourn and let go, looking forward instead to the joyous new season and things in my life which You will spring forth. Please close the doors You want closed and open the doors You want opened. I give You full permission to do this in my life. I ask for wisdom, discernment, and guidance from You, Father. I rest, Father, in Your care. Thank You, Father. In the name of Jesus, I pray. Amen.

DAY 27

THE PROMISES OF GOD

*For all the promises of God in him (Jesus) are "Yes"
and in him (Jesus) "Amen," to the glory of God by us.*
—*2 Corinthians 1:20*

Y ou are reassured by God that you can trust Him. In His Word, it declares that with absolute certainty that whatever God said He will do or promised you, know it will be done (2 Corinthians 1:20). By faith you can be certain and trust that it is already done in the Spirit realm, even before it manifests in your physical reality. You are guaranteed you will receive blessings in (Him), Christ Jesus, basically because of what Jesus did already when He was sacrificed for you on the cross. The promises of God are based on Jesus' righteous sacrifice, His obedience, His goodness, and His character—not on your own. Therefore, if you experience anxiety or question whether God will bless you, His Word and promise is, "Yes." He will fulfill His promises to you and bring them to pass, in Christ Jesus! He will abundantly provide every blessing. The sacrifice and offering of His Son, Jesus, in your place, guarantees you will be blessed because of Christ Jesus' sacrifice.

Now that you realize that God plans to keep His promises, do you know what some of those promises are? There are many promises that God has made to His children because of Jesus. Let me first clarify who God's children are and what this means. Who are His children? First-John 3:1-2 clarifies this. It says, "See what love the Father has given us, that we should be called children of God, and that is what we are . . . Beloved, we are God's children now." Yes, you and all who by faith believe in Christ Jesus and accept Him as their personal Lord and Savior, are now God's children. You who believe, have received the Spirit of adoption, through Christ, and are now admitted into the family of God, who is now your Father (Romans 8:15).

You are one with Jesus, righteous, glorified, justified, redeemed, and reconciled to God, through Christ Jesus (Romans 7:4-6, 1 Corinthians 6:17, 2 Corinthians 5:21, 2 Corinthians 5:18, Romans 8:17, Romans 3:24-25). You are also a joint heir with Christ (Romans 8:16-17). It is all made effective through your faith (Romans 3:25). By one man's (Jesus') act of righteousness, you have justification, life, and blessings, and are now children of the promises of God (Romans 5:18). You should know, however, that the promises of God depend on your faith, in order that the promises may rest on the grace of God, not the law or your personal efforts and goodness (Romans 4:16). God's promises are realized through your faith.

The free gift of righteousness, which you have received from Christ, released you from condemnation due to Adam's sin. Through Christ Jesus and His act of righteousness, you were justified and given life (Romans 5:17-18). You are now, therefore justified by God's grace, as a gift, through the redemption that is in Christ Jesus. God offered Jesus as the sacrifice of atonement by the shedding of His blood, for you (Romans 3:24-25). Christ suffered the punishment you deserved under the law. Therefore, God declared, "I will forgive their iniquity and I will remember their sin no more," because Jesus has fulfilled the law and suffered punishment and death on your behalf (Jerimiah 31:34). It is all made effective through your faith in Jesus (Romans 3:26).

Therefore, Christ has set you free (Galatians 5:1). You could never be justified before God by the law, being unable to obey all things written in the law (Galatians 3:11). However, Jesus has redeemed us all from the curse of the law by becoming a curse for us when He took our sins and was crucified in our place (Galatians 3:13). The law required you to perform perfectly in observing and obeying all that is written in the law, in order to be justified, righteous, saved, and to inherit the promises of God. That proving impossible, however, for you to accomplish on your own, Christ Jesus accomplished it for you, by fulfilling the law and becoming sin for you (2 Corinthians 5:21). Your justification, righteousness, redemption, salvation, and the promises of God are fulfilled and accomplished through Christ. You receive the promise of the Spirit, justification, righteousness, redemption, salvation, and all the promises of God through faith (Galatians 3:11-14). All you have to do to receive it all is to live by faith in the Son of God, Christ Jesus, not through works and your own self-effort. Believe! This is the gift of the grace of God.

You are free from the flesh and, therefore, from sin, death, guilt, condemnation, punishment, jealousy, fear, anxiety, sadness, anger, envy, and whatever tempts you by promising to fill your emptiness, loneliness, desire, thirst, hunger, need, and longing, so that you can feel loved, good enough, worthy, and purposeful (Galatians 5:19–21). When Christ Jesus set you free from the law and the power of sin over you, He set you free to no longer have to submit to the demands and power of sin to dictate, manipulate, and control your thoughts, behaviors, actions, and relationships. Now you are free to live by the Spirit and be guided by the Spirit, instead of sin and needs, passions and desires of the flesh (Galatians 5:24–25).

To protect you, so that you do not give up your freedom attained through Christ, by grace, and submit to the yolk of slavery again (sin, needs, passions, and desires of the flesh), you can now live a life based on the fruit of the Spirit (Galatians 5:1). What is the fruit of the Spirit? It is love, joy, peace, patience, kindness, generosity, faithfulness, gentleness, and self-control (Galatians 5:1). Your worth, value, identity, righteousness, justification, and promises of God are all based on Christ Jesus, and fulfilled and complete in Him. Your faith in Christ is all that is needed to receive these things. You are already loved, blessed, and fulfilled through Christ and your relationship with God. Therefore, you are free now to be filled with love, joy, peace, patience, kindness, generosity, faithfulness, gentleness, and self-control, knowing all things will be received by faith in Christ. Focus your thoughts, behaviors, actions, functioning, and entire being around love, joy, peace, patience, kindness, generosity, faithfulness, gentleness, and self-control. Let these things feed your spirit and hopefulness.

By grace you have been saved through faith because God, who is rich in mercy, out of great love made you alive together with

Christ and brought you near by the blood of Christ (Ephesians 2:8, Ephesians 2:4–5, Ephesians 2:13). Although disappointments and painful circumstances never end, you must endure, remain consistent, and believe that positive, good, and hopeful outcomes will come because of your faith in Christ Jesus and what He accomplished on your behalf. You are surrounded each day by God's love and grace. Therefore, you can purposefully and confidently center and direct your focus and entire being around love, joy, peace, patience, kindness, generosity, faithfulness, gentleness, and self-control, knowing that no matter the challenges, losses, and difficulties you are faced with, God offers you grace and mercy and cares for and watches over you.

Your past disappointments, sins, passions, and desires do not have to control your life, thoughts, behaviors, outcomes, and future, or burden you any longer. They do not have the power to cancel God's plans for your life or the promises of God, made in Christ Jesus. God is merciful, gracious, and compassionate toward His children, all of whom He loves forever (Psalm 103:1–17). Therefore, you will receive all the promises, benefits, rights, and privileges of the children of God in Christ.

It may be comforting to know that, as a child of God, you have received His guarantee of many promises of blessings, and favor. There are numerous promises and blessings made to God's children because of Jesus. A short listing includes promises of love, forgiveness for all your sins, peace, salvation, the Holy Spirit, everlasting life, comfort, joy, freedom, growth, spiritual maturity, healing, encouragement, excellence, strength, courage, God's presence, your answered prayers, provision, prosperity, protection, to do you no harm, hope, a good future, and a destiny to the glory of God. He promises to help you when you struggle with anxiety, fearfulness, guilt, grief, loss, dejectedness, sadness, disappointment, persecution, sickness, disease, uncertainty, being attacked by your enemies, misfortunes, impatience, confusion, temptation, weakness, desires of the flesh, lack of obedience, lack of wisdom and discernment, failure, doubt, condemnation, judgment, and are in any kind of need or suffering in any way. God promises you will receive His help and blessings no matter what you suffer or experience in this life. He offers you a quality life to receive today, filled with fulfillment, joy, and happiness. This includes good relationships and a loving marriage. Let's take a closer look at four specific promises that God has made to His children.

The first promise we will look at is the most powerful and beautiful one of all. It is God's promise to love you with unconditional love. When you reflect on this, all your own anxiety and self-loathing will fade away. God loves you and cares about you, no matter what. His love for you is not based on your own actions, performance, or behaviors. God loved you so much that He sent His own Son, Jesus, to die for you while we were yet sinners (John 3:16). His love endures and goes through all the disappointments, difficulties, and painful experiences with you over the course of your life. His love remains consistent and never ends.

In Christ Jesus, you have received righteousness and separation from sin and the consequences of sin. Therefore, you can rest, knowing that because of Jesus you are forgiven, and by grace you will never be punished and condemned. God loved you with so much great love that He sent His Son, Jesus, and offered Him as a sacrifice for you so that you would not be condemned (John

3:16–17, Ephesians 2:4–5). This is the quality of God's great, unconditional love for you.

God's love for you is so beautiful. This is how it is described, "For I am convinced that neither death, nor life, neither angels, nor rulers, nor things present, nor things to come, nor powers, nor height, nor depth, nor anything else in all creation, will be able to separate us from the love of God in Christ Jesus our Lord." (Romans 8:38–39) Nothing is left out, meaning the love you receive from God is limitless and will last forever. He loves you consistently, faithfully, and forever. You need never fear or become anxious when it comes to His love for you. No circumstance, situation, or anything you have done or failed to do will make God love you less. You are unconditionally loved forever. You can be confident that you can always go to Him just as you really are and experience His comforting, warm, and welcoming, unconditional love.

God has also made you a promise of prosperity. In Jeremiah 29:11 it says, "For I know the plans I have for you. Plans to prosper you and not harm you, plans to give you hope and a future." Yes, God wants you to be prosperous. God has a heart of love that wants to give you His very best and prosper you. This promise of prosperity extends beyond the promise of financial wealth. It also applies to having rich and fulfilling relationships, as well as prosperity in all areas of your life. This includes plans for your life, destiny, purpose, and positive solutions to problems and challenges.

God has personally given careful thought to making plans for you, putting His plans in motion, and setting up a life for you that will provide you with bountiful blessings and solutions to any problem you may ever experience. It is important that you understand that He is the one who plans to achieve it on your behalf. Remember, His promises are not based on your performance, hard work, tireless striving, and how good you are. His promises—including promises of solutions to problems, fulfilling relationships, financial wealth, and everything you need in all areas of your life—are based on Jesus. As it says in His Word, the promises of God are, "Yes" in Christ, and so, through Christ, you only simply say, "Amen," knowing that you will receive the promises of God because of Christ (2 Corinthians 1:20). This is the grace of God. He provides and you receive.

God loves you and cares about you because you are His beloved child (1 John 3:1). His plans are to bless you and give you good things and a life that is full and blessed. His plans for you are for your good and are always what is best and perfect for you. You do not have to see them or know what they are in advance. Simply remember that God loves you and, because He loves you, He will supply all your needs according to the riches of His glory in Christ (Philippians 4:19).

Therefore, you do not have to experience anxiety or work so hard to receive His blessings. His plans will unfold in your life by grace. Grace is based on His love for you and the finished work of Christ Jesus, through whom all your needs will be supplied and met. This means you can relax and follow the path God leads you to, knowing you will be prosperous and blessed. Therefore, do not be anxious about anything but instead, with prayer, supplication, and thanksgiving, make your requests to God (Philippians 4:6).

You can confidently pray with thanksgiving because you know God has promised He will answer and you will receive what is best for your life, by grace, through Christ Jesus. You are also reassured that once you pray to God, His peace will guard your heart and mind in Christ Jesus (Philippians 4:7). When you center your thoughts around the love of God and the grace you have received through Christ, you can be positive that everything will be okay, no matter what your present experience may be. "Amen."

Another promise of God that you are entitled to is to have strength and power by grace, through Christ Jesus. Recognize the far-reaching impact of this blessing which you have received as a child of God, in Christ. Apostle Paul confidently states, "I can do all things through Christ who strengthens me" (Philippians 4:13). The same applies entirely to you. In all circumstances and whatever you must do, you have received the promise that Jesus is your helper. He is the source of your strength, energy, and capacity in all circumstances and all things. It does not matter how weak, deficient, or incapable you feel; look to Jesus instead of yourself. Permit the power of Christ to dwell in you. He is your perfectly strong, able, powerful, and capable source of everything you need, by grace.

This means that by grace, which you have through Christ Jesus, you can always rest and rely on Jesus and receive through Him strength and power (2 Corinthians 12:9–10). This is what it means when Christ told Paul, "My grace is sufficient for you, for power is made perfect in weakness" (2 Corinthians 12:9). The Lord encouraged Paul to tap into His power and strength always, instead of doing it by his own human ability, effort, strength, and power. You can do the same. You do not have to go it alone, either. His power will strengthen you, propel you forward, energize you, and supply all you need. If you try to be your own power source, you will always hit a wall and feel limited and exhausted. When you tap into Jesus' power supply, you will always feel refreshed, stronger, and more powerful. However, this will flow from Jesus, and so you will never feel like you are running out of resources. It is not you who is causing the power to flow or creating it. You simply benefit from receiving and being constantly recharged, refreshed, and strengthened by Him. Jesus is never empty or deficient.

The last promise we will look at is God's promise of protection. God promises to protect and preserve you. He shows in His Word that He did not withhold His own beloved Son, Jesus, to save you from death (John 3:16-17). You were offered the promise of the hope of His glory, through His Son, Jesus, because He loves you so much. Christ Jesus took on mortal form, suffered in His body, and died for you to—protect you. But God has also promised to protect you and keep you safe here and now, in your mortal bodies. He has promised to keep you close to Him, in the secret place of the Most High and to offer you refuge and protection from all enemies, harm, and pestilence (Psalm 91). He has also promised to give His angels charge over you to protect you, keep you in all your ways, and bear you up (Psalm 91:11-12). His loving presence is always with you and He promises to deliver you from trouble and grant you long life (Psalm 91:14-16). In fact, He encourages you to never hesitate to call on Him for His protection, knowing that He will always answer you and help you (Psalm 91:15).

You are encouraged to confidently speak in faith the promises of God over your life. In your everyday situations, proclaim the promises of God. Speak to your situation, problems, and challenges, knowing that God's promises are real and that He will do what He has promised to do. Therefore, you can hold fast to the profession (declaration) of your hope (in the promises of God) without wavering because, it is written, "He is faithful that promised" (Hebrews 10:23).

It is important that you recognize that He faithfully promised you that His Word would not return to Him void, but rather it would accomplish what He purposed it to and would succeed in the areas He promised you (Isaiah 55:10–11). What this means is that the promises He has made and the Word He has spoken and written will be fulfilled. When you speak the Word of God and declare the written Word of God, He promises you will see His promises fulfilled in your life. They will spring forth (Isaiah 43:18–19). Therefore, you can have joy and peace knowing that the promises of God are real.

Today's Powerful Thought
God has a heart of unconditional love for
me and wants to abundantly provide for
me, protect me, and strengthen me.

Prayer
Thank You, Father, that You love me unconditionally.
I am so grateful that You also abundantly supply all
my needs, protect me, and provide me with strength,
by grace, through Your Son, Jesus. Abba Father, thank
You that You provide Your very best right now for
my good. I look forward to a good life full of good
days because You love me, and by grace I benefit

from Jesus' goodness, obedience, and His sacrifice on the cross for me. Thank You for loving me so much more than I can ever comprehend or even deserve. I am grateful I don't have to do it all by myself anymore, because of Jesus. Father, I am so deeply grateful that You show me mercy and compassion, and protect me from all dangers and harm. Thank You for Your angels who protect me and actively safeguard me. In the name of Jesus, I pray. Amen.

DAY 28

GUARD YOUR BELIEFS

During difficult times, such as when praying for a husband or when trying to walk by faith, it may be hard to control your reactions. When your prayers have not been answered as yet, or when you suffer uncertainty, disappointment, and loss, or circumstances seem outside your power and control, you may find yourself struggling to maintain a sense of stability and control over your actions, behaviors, and emotions. During these times, it is easy to feel overwhelmed by intense feelings, such as, anxiety, fear, hopelessness, loneliness, and sadness. Therefore, in these difficult moments it is particularly necessary to focus on what you believe.

We are told that simply by believing God, it was counted to Abraham as righteousness (Genesis 15:6). Yes, God so esteemed the quality of Abraham's belief in Him and His promises, that He equated it as equal to righteousness on Abraham's part. Matthew (8:13) further demonstrates how powerful your beliefs are. Jesus said to the centurion who had a sick servant and was asking for healing, "As thou (you) have believed, so be it done unto you." Through the centurion's belief in Jesus being able and willing to heal, the servant was healed, although he was a great distance away, and Jesus never even saw or touched him. This is the power of what you believe.

Likewise, whether you are aware of it or not, your beliefs will determine your emotions, actions, and the quality of your life, as well as the outcomes you experience in your life. You will find that the quality of your beliefs has the power to positively or negatively impact the quality and course of your life. For example, if you have wrong or inaccurate beliefs, you may feel unlovable, unwanted, powerless, hopeless, anxious, fearful, and depressed. You may also experience feeling trapped in a negative spiral of thinking, which makes you feel hopeless and unable to move forward or make an impact. You may even find that you may not be able to function at the level life demands or navigate mature, adult responsibilities and attain significant mature, adult milestones. Feeling crippled and inflicted with emotional pain, you may consequently sabotage the life God intends for you to enjoy because you are manipulated by false beliefs.

Your beliefs will generate your go-to thoughts or the ones you find yourself repeating in your head or out loud. Your beliefs and the thoughts they generate will, likewise, impact your emotions, choices, actions, and behaviors. You will likely not be able to effectively control and regulate your emotions and maintain a stable emotional world for yourself unless you first control your beliefs and the thoughts they generate. When you struggle to control your emotions, feelings, and actions, it likely indicates that you are experiencing deficiencies in your core belief system.

There may be many reasons to explain why this happens. The most basic reason points to the absence of a clear and well-defined core belief system, based on a solid foundation of truth. Another reason is that you may struggle to activate or maintain a stable core belief system when facing stressful and difficult circumstances. This means that you may struggle with what you believe or that you may experience a crisis of faith. Of course, your faith, at the core, is grounded in what you fundamentally believe.

If you don't have an established belief system, or you question what you ultimately believe, then you will have difficulty maintaining faith. It is easy to struggle, question your beliefs, and experience doubts and fears when you do not have confidence in your beliefs. Therefore, you need to establish a confident belief system and guard the quality of your belief system by intentionally focusing your thoughts on the Word of God.

When you focus your thoughts on the Word of God, you will feel more grounded in your beliefs and experience feeling more loved, cared for, protected, provided for, stable, reinforced, and built up. Let the Word of God sustain you by studying the written Word. Seek other resources as well, like devotionals, pastoral leadership, Christian mentorship and fellowship, and ministries of faith that believe in Christ Jesus and focus on God's Word.

Study the lessons Jesus taught and anchor yourself in the Word of faith based on the love of God and His grace, displayed through the sacrifice of His only begotten Son for you and all the world. Of course, make the Bible your number one go-to resource. The truth contained in the Bible is the foundational resource for your belief. Also, seek guidance from the Holy Spirit and ask God for wisdom, revelation, enlightenment, understanding, insight, clarity, and discernment. Ephesians 1:17–21 offers a prayer you may say when asking God for these things.

You will be surprised by how many unchecked thoughts go through your mind in just one minute. When you actively take control over your thoughts, by focusing them on the Word of God, you will escape the thinking traps and cognitive mazes which keep you bound in fears of love, low self-esteem, worthlessness, depression, guilt, shame, failure, isolation, anger, negative behaviors, negative interpersonal patterns, condemnation, and other negative emotions and patterns. Further, when you occupy yourself with thoughts, based on the Word of God, this will engender a richer and healthier emotional space and positive action and outcome.

This is what it means to bring every thought into captivity (2 Corinthians 10:5). You are also reminded to bring your thoughts into captivity by focusing on Christ in your thought life. As you reflect on Christ, generate core beliefs based on what the Word says about your relationship with Christ Jesus, including the love, grace, righteousness, salvation, provision, favor, blessings, protection, peace, joy, new Spirit, nature, and new identity you have received through Christ. Focus on being a beloved child of God through Christ. Once you generate thoughts that focus on God's Word, your relationship with Christ Jesus, and God's love, you will find you no longer suffer from crippling doubts, fears, and negative emotions.

It is written, "I believed and so I spoke" (2 Corinthians 4:13). The apostle Paul encouraged you to focus on the Word and speak out loud what you believe by the Spirit of faith. Spoken words must be centered around your core beliefs, based on the Word of God. Every thought and every word that comes out of your mouth, as much as possible, must be brought into submission. While this may sound difficult, with practice and time, it will become easier and more automatic. Jesus Himself said, "Truly I tell you, if you say to this mountain be taken up and thrown into the sea, and if you do not doubt in your heart, but believe that what you say will come to pass, it will be done for you" (Mark 11:23). His words indicate that, as a child of God, your words spoken in faith, based on the Word of God, are powerful.

Aligning your core beliefs, thoughts, and speech with the Word of God is a powerful tool to use in spiritual warfare. The mystery of the gospel reveals that the Word of God is the sword of the Spirit and part of God's protective armor for you to be able to stand against the wiles of the devil during spiritual warfare (Ephesians 4:11, 4:17). When you base your beliefs, thoughts, and spoken words on the Word of God, you will also feel more secure in the knowledge that, by grace, you are already victorious through Christ and His finished work on the cross.

Therefore, you don't have to fear the enemy's attacks and mind games. Jesus defeated your enemies and, by grace, He fights your battles and provides for you. He is your fortress in difficult times (Psalm 91). He promised to be your strength when you feel tired, weak, unable to carry burdens, and are involved in a spiritual battle (2 Corinthians 12:9–10). Based on His finished work on the cross, you can rest in the armor of God. Therefore, operate in faith and let yourself rest in the power of God's armor by speaking words based on the Word of God, which is the sword of the Spirit. Speak out loud what you believe, without compromising. When you do so, expect positive results.

When you are going through a situation in life, experiencing fear and doubt, facing a challenge, or going through a spiritual battle, you can also use the written Word in the way Jesus demonstrated when He was tempted by the devil (Matthew 4:1–11). Instead of responding by giving in to emotions and temptation, Jesus quoted the written Word of God out loud. He said, "It is written," and went on to quote scripture (Matthew 4:4). What Jesus demonstrated is what you can also do, which is to stand on the Word of God by speaking His written Word and prefacing it by first saying, "It is written." When you say this, you allow God's authority, divinity, power, strength, love, grace, peace, truth, promises, wisdom, and victory to flow into your situation and through you. You also place the focus directly on God and Jesus, instead of on yourself.

You never have to do it by your own authority, self-effort, and striving. Let God do it for you. You are not alone. Let God's written Word be your response for every situation and emotion you are challenged or need help with. Memorize passages of scripture which address common themes you face, such as related to God's love, grace, the promises of God to believers, God's protection, victory in God, fear, and worry. Write them down, keep them close, and remember to say, "It is written."

Align all three—your core beliefs, thoughts and the words you speak—all based and anchored on the Word of God, to have the most powerful impact. Do this and let the grace of God take effect, through Jesus, in winning that spiritual battle for you and helping you in the daily affairs of life, including in the area of love and relationships. You don't have to struggle so hard or do it by yourself.

Today's Powerful Thought

When I align my beliefs, thoughts, and spoken words with the Word of God, life is so much better, and my challenges don't seem impossible or too much to bear.

Prayer

Help me, Abba Father, to not be consumed by negative, pessimistic, condemning, anxious, fearful, doubtful, critical, sad, hopeless, and self-destructive thoughts. Help me to instead focus on Your Word and on Your Son, Jesus. Help me to align my beliefs, thoughts, and spoken words with Your Word of truth. I receive Your love and grace, which anchor me and help me to guard my beliefs and thoughts. I am grateful that I am Your beloved child, through Jesus. In the name of Jesus, I pray. Amen.

DAY 29

LOVE: CORE BELIEF NUMBER ONE

In moments when you experience emotional distress, and do not feel loved or worthy of love, you may find yourself driven by desire to reach for someone else so you can feel loved or less alone. To achieve this, you may respond in ways which seem out of character for you, or which are not consistent with your beliefs. You may even engage in behaviors which seem out of your personal control. These are the moments when you are most susceptible to acting impulsively and to being manipulated and controlled by desire and need. You may be tempted to settle for less than God intends for you. In these moments it is especially important that you focus your thoughts on God's love for you. This is grounding belief number one, and a most wonderful and powerful acknowledgement of truth. God loves you unconditionally. Consciously focus your thoughts on this powerful and liberating truth. Occupy your every thought and moment with it. Let it become the background music to your life.

You can, with fullest confidence, believe that God loves you unconditionally. "For God so loved the world that He gave His only begotten Son, that whosoever believeth in Him should not perish, but have everlasting life" (John 3:16). This is regarded as a foundational scripture that points to the best and most perfect love possible. It also reveals just how much you are valued and cared for by God. In your reflections on this scripture, make it a personal statement of belief. What does this mean? Basically, personalize it into a statement about God's love for you. Here is an example of what I mean. Based on John (3:16–17), you can say out loud or in your mind, "God so loves me that He gave His only begotten Son for me, so that I would be saved. He didn't send His Son, Jesus, into the world to condemn me, but only so that I would be saved and have life through Jesus." You may also summarize it this way, "God doesn't want to condemn me or punish me. He loves me. Jesus took all my punishment already."

Belief in God's unconditional love for you is a beautiful core belief on which you can organize your entire faith belief system. It acknowledges the ever-present, faithful, everlasting, unconditional, and perfect love that God feels deeply for you and freely gives you. His love is a gift. You do not have to do anything to attain it or maintain it. This basic truth tells you that as a person loved by God the Father, you are deeply cared about, and your overall welfare and happiness are always important to God. Yes, you are so very special and important to Him and He loves you so much that He sacrificed His own Son, Jesus, to save you. He loves you so much that He offered you grace, through Jesus. This is what your relationship with God is based on. He loves you unconditionally and does not want to condemn you. He will do anything to save you, protect you, and ensure you have a good life. By not withholding Jesus from being sacrificed in order to save you, He proved this (Romans 8:32). This certainly lets you know that you are a priority to God because He loves you. You don't have to get stuck in trying to figure it out or complicate the facts; simply accept this basic truth—God loves you.

His love is a fortress when facing difficult times. God sees your struggle and your pain. He loves you unconditionally and is there for you. His unconditional love says, "I am with you and I love you. I will strengthen you and help you. Have peace, I have overcome the world" (John 3:16, Isaiah 41:10, Matthew 28:20, John 16:33). You are asked to believe you are God's beloved child and He will always be there to help you, protect you, provide for you, offer you safety and security, and give you strength (1 John 3:1).

I love the way the Song of Solomon (2:4) talks about God and Jesus' love for us. It says, "He brought me to the banqueting house and his banner over me was love." The imagery of the banquet, the house, feast, and banner of love signify how God welcomes you home to Him with unconditional love, compassion, warmth, joy, and celebration. He withholds nothing, but instead provides everything lovingly, freely, and generously. He is your loving Father. This is not based on what you deserved or earned by your own merit and efforts. It is freely bestowed. Picture the Father's welcoming arms stretched out to you with unconditional love. Recognize also that the banner of God's love is a symbol of how God unconditionally, lovingly, and compassionately covers, protects, and provides for you. It is His assurance that you will receive love, shelter, provision, and protection, as a member of His household and family. The banner also symbolizes that you, as a believer in Christ Jesus as your Savior, have received the gift of righteousness through Christ. You are covered in His righteousness. The verse further provides the imagery of wealth, grandeur, majesty, opulence, comfort, overflow, overabundance, and provision. This all signifies how richly you are unconditionally loved.

In case you still wonder just how much you are loved, Jesus clarified this. He revealed that God loves you to the same (or equal) measure to which God loves Him, Jesus, His beloved and only begotten Son (John 17: 23). You are also a most beloved child in Christ. While this may be difficult to comprehend, recognize what a tremendous outpouring of unconditional love God bestows upon you. He loves you equally as Jesus, His most beloved, perfect, righteous, and obedient Son. Therefore, in truth, His love for you is beyond measurable quantity or anything you can imagine possible. Meditate on His love for you, draw nearer, and feel His overflowing, unconditional love.

As you focus your thoughts on God's unconditional love for you and meditate on how much He loves you, allow the presence of His love to relieve distress and fill the void. Anchor yourself in God's love. Know that you are not alone or abandoned. Sit quietly and invite His presence, feeling how deeply He loves you. You may simply say, "Abba Father please help me to feel Your presence and Your love for me."

When you are stressed and facing challenges, you may question His love for you. You may even question if what you believe is true. In this state, you may find yourself seeking answers in other places and, perhaps, even consider doing it the way others in the world do it. To put it plainly, you may seek fulfillment in your flesh and instant gratification. Inevitably, you will experience only temporary and false relief and satisfaction. In the end, you will not find real love. During these times, focus on this core belief—God loves you unconditionally.

Today's Powerful Thought
God loves me unconditionally and
His banner over me is love!

Prayer
Father, thank You that You love me unconditionally. I focus right now on Your love for me and ask You to help me feel Your loving presence. Help me, Father, to focus my thoughts on the free gift of Your unconditional love. During times of anxiety, uncertainty, crisis, fear, loneliness, and feeling unloved, help me to focus on Your unconditional love. I realize I don't have to do anything to deserve Your love and that You sacrificed Your Son, Jesus, for me. I realize that I am valued and loved forever and will never be condemned. In the name of Jesus, I pray. Amen.

DAY 30

GRACE: CORE BELIEF NUMBER TWO

Another powerful core belief, right after the truth of God's love for you, is the gift of His grace. Through grace, you are set free forever. Grace invites you to not be preoccupied with your own efforts and goodness, but to focus completely on the gift of grace you receive through Christ Jesus. Grace through Jesus frees you from the curses, condemnation, and punishment you would have received because of the law (Galatians 3:13–14).

Through faith in Christ Jesus, you have been redeemed from the law, justified, and also received the blessings of Abraham, by grace (Galatians 2:21, Galatians 3:13–14). Jesus satisfied your requirements by fulfilling the law and then He took your sins into Himself, gave you righteousness, and paid the penalty for your sin for you. You are free because of Christ. It is all by grace.

As a believer in Christ, as your personal Savior and Lord, you are at liberty from sin, condemnation, and death (Romans 8:1). By grace, you have received the gift of salvation and the righteousness of God through Christ (2 Corinthians 5:21). You are declared righteous now, through Christ. Sometimes you may feel ashamed or guilty and reason that you deserve to be punished. You may expect condemnation and punishment because of the judgment and lack of love of others, or because of what you have been taught before. You may also reason that it is expected that everyone needs to apply extra effort and work hard. However, by God's grace, through the finished work of Christ Jesus on the cross at Calvary, you are permanently and forever free from the law, sin, judgment, condemnation, and punishment (Galatians 2:21, Galatians 5:4). Jesus beautifully demonstrated this grace when He was speaking to the woman compromised by sin and brought before Him for judgment. He said, "Neither do I condemn you" (John 8:11). He refused to punish her and set her free from condemnation, sin, and death.

Like this woman, you have also been discharged from the law, which held you captive, and are now free and have received a new life in the Spirit (Romans 7:6). Christ Jesus has set you free from the law of sin and death (Romans 8:1). God, who is rich in mercy, out of great love made us—who were dead because of sin—alive together with Christ and saved us by grace (Ephesians 2:3–5). Not only did God raise us from death with Christ, but He also seated us with Christ in heavenly places, all because of His grace toward us (Ephesians 2:6–7). You are saved by grace through faith and not by your own efforts and works (Ephesians 2:9). It is by grace, because all of this is a gift from God.

You are reminded that it is no more grace if you have to work to be justified and attain forgiveness, righteousness, salvation, blessings, favor, and the help of God to overcome challenges, problems, and spiritual attacks (Romans 11:6). You are saved and brought near, being made one with Christ and a child of God by the blood of Christ, all through grace (Ephesians 2:13, 1 Corinthians 6:17). This is a great reminder that your own personal efforts and hard work will not be sufficient in attaining personal fulfillment or love.

You do not have to work and struggle so hard to attain God's best for your life, including a loving relationship with a mate. You are reminded that if it is attained by your works, then it is no more grace. It is also not based on your goodness. It all comes through God's grace and love. By grace, your worth, value, and goodness are based on the righteousness you received from Christ Jesus and on His goodness and obedience. By God's grace it is all accomplished and granted freely to you through Christ Jesus. Yes, it is totally undeserved and not based on a reward system or on your personal efforts and accomplishments.

I encourage you not to continue questioning why God did this or reflecting backwards to all your mistakes, bad choices, and the consequences you suffered. Place your focus instead on grace and the freedom, blessings, and favors it offers you today. Focus instead on Christ Jesus and what He deserves and what you receive through Him by grace. When you feel overwhelmed, condemned, unworthy, hopeless, and undeserving, simply ask yourself this question: Is Jesus worthy, deserving, good enough, loved, favored, blessed, physically and emotionally healthy, rich, powerful, and free? By grace and the love of God, as He (Jesus) is, so are you in this world (1 John 4:17). Remember, that by grace, it is all based on Jesus and not on you. Rest in the peace this brings in knowing that grace sets you free to receive every good thing that Jesus deserves.

Through the grace of God, you also receive help and protection. He is your shield (Proverbs 30:5). He also offers you eternal comfort, good hope, and strengthens your heart in every good work and word, through grace (2 Thessalonians 2:16-17). Remember, you are not in this alone; God and Jesus are with you and on your side. Grace also means that you have a good shepherd who looks out for you and protects you. Through grace, you can rest and not struggle so hard. You can be confident that in Christ Jesus you have a personal advocate, Savior, and friend. Jesus loves you, and you can enjoy the satisfaction of knowing you never have to go it alone again. He will guide you to the right people, good situations, and the best solutions. He will watch over you, fight your battles for you, and protect you. He is your good shepherd, who laid down His life for you and in whom you now have everlasting life (Psalm 23, John 10:10-11). You can rest in His strength and wisdom, as He guides you and does what is necessary on your behalf.

At times, you may find that stress, fatigue, a memory, painful circumstances, other people, or negative emotions may start a negative spiral of thoughts and emotions. This can make you feel guilty, ashamed, alone, sad, fearful, unworthy, condemned, hopeless, and unloved. During these times, the enemy wants you to fail to recognize that the grace of God and the finished work of Jesus gives you victory over your circumstances and all the troubles and problems you are experiencing.

To win this battle of your mind and break every chain that tries to bind you, focus on God's unconditional love and grace toward you and the favor you receive through the obedience of Christ Jesus and His finished work on the cross at Calvary. You don't deserve to suffer, live at a level less than God's best for His children, or be bounded by emotional problems, because God loves you unconditionally and the grace of God ensures that you will have a quality life and live it more abundantly because of Christ (John 10:10, 1 Timothy 1:15–16). You are assured that the grace, mercy, and love of God always overflow, no matter what you have done or failed to do (1 Timothy 1:13–16). Simply believe and fully accept His grace, even when you struggle with negative thoughts and emotions.

Today's Powerful Thought
I am saved and will have a good life because of the grace of God, through Christ Jesus.

Prayer
Father, thank You for Your grace and the sacrifice of Your Son, Jesus, for me. Thank You that I don't have to struggle so hard on my own or try to be perfect anymore. I am so grateful I can rest in this gift of Your grace and not feel unworthy, alone, weak, condemned, and hopeless. Thank You that Your grace is not based on how good I am or what I deserve, but by grace, I am blessed based on Jesus, who is my good shepherd who loves, takes care of, looks out for, provides for, and protects me. Thank You for the good life and good relationships I will receive because of Your grace. In the name of Jesus, I pray. Amen.

DAY 31

I BELIEVE GOD

Just what is the right perspective when praying for love with a mate and dealing with loneliness, anxiety, or hopelessness? What should you do when you wonder if God will be there for you, to help you and offer you guidance and the right direction? What is the right approach when you desperately struggle with faith and being able to manage your challenges and disappointments, or when the road seems so exhausting, disheartening, and unpredictable? Do you doubt? Have you given up on hoping for love?

Make an intentional choice to believe with deepest conviction, and to anchor your faith and hope in one supreme core belief: "I believe God." "I believe God," is a statement of absolute, unwavering, unquestioning belief in God without doubt. It is a statement of absolute trust in God. It is a statement of absolute faith in God. It is an orientation of absolute faith and trust in His Word, no matter what. It is impossible to simultaneously believe God and His Word, while also experiencing hopelessness at the same time.

What else does this belief imply? It is the powerful and strong conviction that God is real. It is a strong statement of belief that God is who He says He is, He will do what He says He will, and

His Word is true. Therefore, you can confidently believe what is written in God's Word about His love for you, His grace, His Son Jesus, His protection, His provision, and all His promises. It also means that you can believe God's intimate Word to you and the guidance He gives you personally. Further, "I believe God," is a statement which reflects your personal commitment to totally believing and trusting God now, even in the face of disappointment, contrary evidence, or challenging circumstances. It is a commitment to believing God and being obedient to His Word and will. It is a strong commitment to living by your beliefs and to aligning your thoughts, spoken words, and behaviors with your beliefs. It is not truly total commitment until your thoughts, behaviors, and words line up with your belief in God.

This commitment to believe God calls for an entire paradigm shift in the way you see yourself and others. It calls for a paradigm shift in your approach to life and challenges. Such a shift requires that God becomes the center of love, faith, and hope in your life. It is a powerful way to simply overcome the world by believing God and His Word.

"I believe God," is unlike other statements, such as, "I can believe God, I am going to believe God, I pray to be able to trust and believe God more, and I will believe God." These seemingly similar statements of belief have the quality of not fully believing God. They imply that you have not fully believed God or committed to totally believing and trusting Him. They imply hesitation and the qualities of anxiety, distrust, doubt, and fear. These other statements question if God can truly qualify as trustworthy, believable, fully loving toward you, and deeply concerned about your happiness and well-being.

Therefore, statements such as these, not grounded in full unwavering belief in God and His Word, become major obstacles to really believing God, accepting His Word as truth, following His will, and aligning your identity, thoughts, words, and actions with His Word. They also interfere with being able to fully benefit from His love, grace, blessings, and promises to which you are entitled. Sometimes, your failure to believe God blocks the path, keeps the door closed, and is your biggest obstacle or opposition. To overcome, you must put on the shield of faith and ground yourself in the truth, which is based on the Word of God, to maintain your belief (Ephesians 6:13–17).

How does one develop the capacity to fully believe God without any shadow of possible doubt? Fostering a belief in God with deepest conviction is often facilitated by getting to know Him personally, in a genuine and honest connection over time. It comes through engaging in a closer personal relationship with Him. A deeper knowing and trust will develop over time, by going through varying experiences together while consistently feeling loved, cared for, supported, comforted, worthy, important, accepted, and forgiven, no matter what. This is exactly what you can expect from God in a relationship. No matter how difficult this is to believe personally, this is the truth of who God is. He will reveal Himself to you clearly, and you will recognize the truth yourself, once you go to Him and open yourself to the experience of His unconditional love and grace.

God is real, and therefore the experience of His presence and love is real as well. In His presence, you will know who He really is. You will feel whole, fulfilled, complete, and filled with a sense of peace. You will also feel freer to be emotionally vulnerable, honest, genuine, and open, as you experience His love in a safe relationship with Him, which provides a safe space of no fear of rejection, criticism, judgment, punishment, or condemnation. This is the space of deeper knowing that comes from personally getting to experience God in a closer, personal relationship. He loves you and is there for you, despite how difficult and painful life is, the problems and disappointments you face, and the mistakes you have made. You will experience His love, faithfulness, compassion, understanding, and hopefulness, as He helps you through life's misfortunes and suffering, protects you, and provides for you.

God has also provided a beautiful way to communicate directly with Him in the Spirit. Those who speak in tongues speak directly to God (1 Corinthians 14:2). If you speak in tongues, you are not speaking to other people, but instead, it is a direct communication link with God. The spiritual gift of speaking in tongues is instrumental in building up, strengthening, encouraging, and consoling your own spirit, mind, and body via this direct communication with the Father (1 Corinthians 14:4). You are edified when you speak in tongues to communicate directly to God. In this intimate communication in the Spirit, you will receive a sense of peace as you enter God's loving presence and His rest, which builds you up (Isaiah 28:12).

His desire is to give you rest and renew your spirit, body, mind, and emotions. You will feel connected and closer to God in a way you have never experienced before. Certainly, you will also experience His perfect love, as well, because God is love. During this intimate communication, God will speak to you (Isaiah 28:11). This powerful, direct communication link with

God is facilitated by the Holy Spirit. You do not have to figure it out by yourself. This intimacy with God and the benefits which follow are all activated by speaking in tongues. It is beautiful. If you want to activate the gift of praying/speaking in tongues, simply pray and ask God for it, similarly as you are instructed to do if you also desire the gift of interpretation of tongues (1 Corinthians 14:13). Believe and you will receive it. All believers are entitled to this gift, by the grace that is in Christ.

You can also simply pray or just talk to God as you would in normal conversation with someone else. No scripted conversation is needed nor any ceremony. You have access to God always as His beloved child. He loves you and wants a real relationship with you. Therefore, He will always respond to you.

Start a conversation with Him, where you hold nothing back and just come as you are, without disguise or hiding. Be honest, genuine, and open, knowing you can be yourself without anxiety and fears. Make a 100 percent commitment to getting to know Him personally and to spending time with Him.

For you to fully experience this deeper, genuine, and honest emotional connection with God, it requires a personal investment and commitment on your part—of placing a relationship with God as a priority in your life. No relationship becomes truly more intimate, deep, and strong unless you do so. God wants a close personal relationship with you, but you must also be willing to truly go deeper and engage with God.

What else will help you to believe God? You can also look to the Word of God to know Him and who He is. He shows Himself in His written Word. You will find His true character and nature of love, grace, faithfulness, compassion, and generosity revealed in His Word. One thing that will be revealed for certain is that because God loves you and wanted to save and bless you, He sacrificed His own Son, Jesus, for you (John 3:16–17). This is how you know you can believe God. The sacrifice of Jesus demonstrated the proof of His great love for you.

Today's Powerful Thought
I believe God one hundred percent!

Prayer
Abba, please help me to experience Your presence, perfect love, and grace now, so that I can fully receive the reassuring peace of believing You and Your Word fully, without anxiety, doubts, fears, and compromising myself. Help me to establish a new perspective, which is grounded in the love You have for me and the grace I have received, through Christ. I believe, Abba Father, that I need not look at any other proof than the sacrifice of Your Son for me to know I can believe You and will receive all Your promises. Thank You, Abba Father. I believe You 100 percent. In the name of Jesus, I pray. Amen!

DAY 32

FOLLOWING THE WILL OF GOD

> *The human mind plans the way but the Lord, directs the steps.*
> —Proverbs 16:9

> *Do not be conformed to this world, but be transformed by the renewing of your minds, so that you may discern what is the will of God—what is good and acceptable and perfect.*
> —Romans 12:2

In seeking to find the right answers and make the right choices, you are encouraged to follow the will of God. Yet you may discover that this is more difficult than anticipated. Each human being is engaged in a constant fleshly battle. The spirit and the flesh are always in conflict and opposed to each other. Paul groaned about the battle between sin in his flesh and his new Spirit in

Christ (Romans 14:25). He said that the wickedness he did not wish to do, he ultimately found himself doing, although his spirit did not long to do it. It is a common struggle for everyone in Christ. Remember, while your spirit has been transformed, your flesh is not yet fully transformed.

You may think you have surrendered to the will of God only to discover your mind plans and leads the way, based on the reasoning of the world and its wisdom, pride, desire, envy, lust, and lack of faith. You may also struggle with wanting a sense of more personal power and control, especially when circumstances are difficult or seem unpredictable and unstable. Of course, every human being must confront the reality of not having absolute control and power over one's own life and situations faced or in the world in general. This can be extremely challenging to accept when also experiencing doubts, a crisis of faith, anxiety, and dread about your future and how things may turn out. You may struggle with wanting to feel like you have a sense of power and control by going the way you desire, which may be contrary to God's will. You may not even be aware that your flesh and human heart and mind are influencing and manipulating your thoughts, emotions, choices, and actions.

So, what does one do? How do you know what God's will is for your life? How do you permit your steps, plans, and actions to be directed by Him? As a function of grace, you need not struggle to work this out on your own. Through grace, you can call on Jesus to help you. He can never be compromised by sin. He already defeated sin on the cross. He is also the good shepherd who will guide you and direct your steps (Psalm 23, John 10:11, Proverbs 16:9). Therefore, voluntarily place yourself under the care of your good shepherd, your loving Lord and Savior, Jesus Christ. Do this by placing yourself in agreement with God by saying, "Yes," to His plans in every area of your life, including the areas of love, relationships, and marriage. Then, by grace, call on Jesus to help you follow His lead.

You are told in Romans (8:7) that it is impossible for your flesh (desires, needs, urges, and cravings) to submit or come into agreement with the ways of God. Therefore, your solution is separate from your own exhaustive efforts to get it right and figure it out on your own. Your solution is to ask for help from God and Jesus. Ask for wisdom and guidance. It will all be accomplished by grace. Instead of being self-focused and preoccupied with the situation you are facing, you are invited to focus on your union with Christ and the grace you have received from God through Him. Focus on Him as your Lord and Savior who, because of the bountiful love and grace of God, was offered as a sacrifice for you to set you free from the bondage and penalty of sin (Romans 5:21). Focus on being one with Christ and being made righteous and justified through Him (1 Corinthians 6:17, Romans 5:18–19). Focus on being a child of God, joint heir with Christ, and glorified with Him (Romans 8:17).

Instead of living in the flesh by your own judgment and efforts and the ways and wisdom of the world, realize the benefits of grace through Christ and that you are justified through Him. For example, instead of living in the flesh, one benefit is that you can now live by faith in the Son of God and by the Spirit of Christ, who lives in you (Galatians 2:20). This means you live by the grace of God. This further means that you have received the benefit of not being separate from Christ in discerning God's will, following God's will, solving problems, knowing the right thing to do, positively living life, and going through storms and challenges. Further, you have an additional helper, the Holy Spirit, who Christ gave you as the Spirit of truth (John 16:7–13).

As your good shepherd, Christ is your protector, helper, strength, and guide. Through the grace of God, everything is accomplished through Christ. You do not have to accomplish it by yourself. It is not really intended that you try to achieve anything without Christ. You are intended to function as one with Jesus. In the same way your identity is in Christ, and your righteous standing and justification cannot be achieved on your own without Him, you are intended to also be aided by Christ in knowing and following the will of God.

Psalms (37:23–24) confirms that help and solutions are provided to you through your relationship with Jesus and His guidance. It says, "The steps of a good man are ordered by the Lord." Further Proverbs (16:9) confirms that the Lord helps you by directing your steps and, in so doing, He, therefore, sets you on the right course. Jesus provides the help you need in following the will of God by putting you on the right course, and directing and ordering your steps, according to the will of God. When you embrace the Spirit of Christ in you and allow yourself to fully function in the grace of God and permit your relationship with Christ to take full effect, you are no longer subject to being led by your flesh, desires, and worldly wisdom. You are not left to do this on your own strength, but rather in connection and relationship with Christ.

Further, even though you may fall or stumble, along the path of following God's will, you will not be completely cast down and without hope, because the Lord will hold you up with His hand

(Psalm 37:24). Therefore, even if you get it wrong, go off track, or fail, Jesus is there to help and assist you so you will experience the good life God wants for you. Jesus helps you to stand on solid ground and move forward. You benefit from Jesus taking your hand, holding you up, and bringing you to safety and back on the right course. He never abandons you. Your stumbling does not matter. God does not punish you but instead He lovingly offers Jesus to help you.

In seeking answers and following God's will for your life, Christ Jesus is your good shepherd and guide, who is revealed in the Psalms as the one you can depend on to protect you and provide for you (Psalm 23). He leads you through the darkness, along the confusing, challenging, and dangerous terrain. He provides you solutions and supplies whatever you need. He gives you rest. He comforts you. He keeps you safe no matter what is going on around you or what you are facing. He showers you with love, goodness, and mercy all the days of your life. His blessings overflow. You are simply asked to let Jesus guide and lead you, while you follow. He removes the obstacles for you. You are not alone. Simply take the opportunity to fully rest in the strength, safety, security, and grace you receive through Christ.

When you rely on Jesus you don't have to struggle on your own to be wise, strong, obedient, and capable of following the will of God and executing the steps needed. Jesus is able to follow God's will for your life, even when you are not. You have received being one in the Spirit with Him, the incorruptible Son of God, who is one with God, knows the Father's will, and is obedient and able to do what is asked on your behalf. Don't try to do it by yourself. Instead, completely become Christ-centered and focused. Accept that He can do what you cannot. Give Jesus the authority to guide and lead your steps in following and executing the perfect will of God. This is functioning in grace and relying on and resting in Christ. Due to God's grace toward you, Jesus is your answer for everything. Now being one in the Spirit, you are asked to rely on Him always. Rest in His ability and power by asking Him to help you follow God's will.

Jesus demonstrated His ability to follow the will of God in the garden of Gethsemane before His crucifixion (Matthew 26:36–39). In the garden, He followed the plan God had set out for His life and prayed that the Father's will be done instead of His own, despite knowing that He would be sacrificed and separated from God. He did not compromise or succumb to temptation, sadness, fear, pride, desire, and need. He did what was needed to save mankind despite the cost to Himself. Therefore, you can be confident in Him as your strength, helper, and guide. Jesus continues to be your infallible solution over the course of your entire life. He is your loving Savior and redeemer.

Therefore, in the midst of your struggle, realize that you can call on Jesus and ask Him directly for help. You can rest and not be caught in the struggle between your flesh and your spirit in following God's way, plan, and directions. With Jesus, you will no longer feel confused, anxious, fearful, unprepared, and incapable. This is operating in the Spirit of Christ that you have received. This is the benefit of God's grace. Your Savior will never fail you.

You are also asked to renew your mind so that you can discern the will of God and know what the good, acceptable, and perfect way of God is (Romans 12:2). Knowing that your mind and heart often want to go contrary to the will of God, one way to renew your mind is to read, concentrate, and meditate on the Word of God. Then use the Word of God as the central focus of your thoughts, beliefs, and spoken words. For example, focus on Christ, your connection with Him, your identity in Him, your inheritance in Him, the grace you have received through Him, and God's sacrifice of Him to save you. You can also focus on the benefits of grace, knowing that sin, punishment, condemnation, and death were already defeated on the cross. Focus on the fact that in whatever area you are concerned about, you have already been declared victorious by the grace you have received through Christ (1 Corinthians 15:57). Focus on the promises of God in Christ and the blessing you receive. Focus on God's perfect, unconditional love for you. Also, take the opportunity to make seeking wisdom from the Word your principle thing, instead of consulting worldly wisdom or being led by your flesh. Further, make sure your spoken words also align with the Word of God. Spoken words based on the Word of God are powerful in renewing the mind.

Recognize that it is necessary to align the words you speak with the Word of God and what you know about God as the source of love, grace, and blessings. You must acknowledge and believe that His will is always wise, beneficial for you, and in your best interests, as well as intended to protect, provide and keep you safe from harm.

In his book, St John Maximovitch of Tobolsk (b. 1651 d. 1715), an archbishop, suggested you must unite the human and divine will by desiring to be always close to God in relationship, but also in your thoughts, actions, the words you speak, and in your heart (2018).[2] He suggested that you follow the example of

Jesus in the garden of Gethsemane at the Mount of Olives, by praying and speaking words which are committed to following God's will (Luke 22:40–44). Simple words like, "Let your will be done Father, for I know it is for my good," or "Let my will be your will and my heart your heart," can bring you into the position of alignment and obedience with whatever God's will is for your life (St John of Tobolsk, 2018). It is an act of permission and cooperation, which facilities agreement between your will and God's will. Even saying the first part of the Lord's Prayer (Thy will be done in earth, as it is in heaven) may be beneficial for this same reason (Matthew 6:9).

Be cautioned, however, that it is a better solution to not work tirelessly by your own efforts or to strive to be perfect. Understand that what pleases God is when you operate and rest in Him and Jesus. A do-do mentality is the mentality of a slave. A focus on receiving by grace is the mentality of a son and daughter in Christ. You have been set free by Christ and His sacrifice on the cross, by the grace of God. In following God's will, you are asked to function in His grace and experience the benefit of the peace of Christ by allowing yourself to be guided and led by Christ. You are simply asked to engage in an act of permission and cooperation.

Let the assurance of God's bountiful grace comfort you, even when you operate outside the will of God or make an error in discerning His will. You are never truly abandoned or lost. God will provide you a way of coming back into His will. He will provide a path that leads to solutions to your problems. He will still bless you and provide a place of shelter, security, safety, protection, provision, the fulfillment of His promises, and blessings.

You are assured of this because you are never cut off from His love and grace. This is demonstrated in numerous passages of scripture all throughout the Bible, which show how God's love, grace, and mercy never run out, as He fulfills His promises and provides many blessings, even to fallen and broken people.

What is God's final Word? Focus on God's love for you and His mercy, evidenced by the sacrifice of His Son, Jesus. This is essential in following the will of God.

Today's Powerful Thought
By grace, I will let Jesus direct my steps, one step at a time, in following the will of God. In being able to do what the Father wills, I will rest in Jesus, who will never fail.

Prayer
Dear Jesus, my merciful Savior, I know I am not able to follow Abba Father's will on my own. Sometimes, I am not able to even discern what His will is. Please help me to know what His will is for me and to follow You as You guide me and direct my steps. Help me to live free in Your Spirit by grace. Protect me and provide for me. Be my strength. Help me to focus on the Father's love and mercy toward me. Thank You for loving me, Lord.

I know I can trust You because You love me and gave Yourself as a sacrifice for me, because it was the Father's will. I also ask for help from the Holy Spirit, as You lead me Lord. Jesus, I know You will always be obedient and are always capable of doing the will of God, our Father. I will therefore rest in You and rely on the Father's love and grace. I will let You accomplish it all for me, Savior, because You cannot fail. Thank You, Abba Father, for loving me so much that You offer me Your Son to help me always. Let it all be according to Your will for me, Abba. In the name of Jesus, I pray. Amen.

DAY 33

FAITH IN ACTION: RESTING IN JESUS

I came not to call the righteous, but sinners to repentance.
—Luke 5:32

Believe ye that I am able to do this?
. . .According to your faith be it unto you.
—Matthew 9:28–29

You who believe have received the abundance of grace and the free gift of righteousness through Christ. It is a free gift of righteousness by grace, which takes effect when you believe that Christ Jesus is your Lord and Savior who was sacrificed on the cross for you so that you would not be condemned for your sins and trespasses but instead be justified through Him and receive everlasting life. It is made effective through your faith in Jesus, who God offered as a sacrifice of atonement by His blood, because God so loved you and wanted to save you. By His abundant grace, God justifies the one who has faith in Jesus. When you believe, through our Lord and Savior Jesus Christ, you are reconciled to God as His beloved and righteous child who is one with and identified with Christ. You are called to simply have faith in Jesus. (Romans 3:24-26, Romans 5:17-19, Romans 5:11).

Once you believe, you may rest in Jesus by focusing your faith, thoughts, and actions on Jesus and the Word of God. Below I have offered some concrete and practical examples on how to do this in everyday life, as you walk forward in the new life you have received in Christ.

<u>Actively Believe By Faith</u>
Believe God by faith. Guard your beliefs by anchoring them in the Word of God.

Believe that God loves you unconditionally, forgives you, and offers you grace and favor. Once you believe in Christ as your Lord and Savior, you become righteous and justified through Him and will no longer be condemned. Therefore, God will not punish you for mistakes you have made, or your past and future sins.

Believe you are loved by Jesus, who died for your sins and that you are one with Him and identified with Him. Believe you are a joint heir with Christ Jesus and are reconciled to God as His beloved child through grace.

Believe you have received the abundance of grace from God.

Believe in the promises of God, which include promises of salvation, blessings, favor, protection, provision, and a hopeful future. Believe that you receive this all freely by God's abundant grace, because He loves you and because of Jesus' sacrifice.

Believe that the promises of God include having a loving

partnership and marriage with a man who believes as you do, in the grace of God through Christ and who will love you as Christ loves the church. Believe love is possible for you. Believe you are worthy of love because you are the righteousness of God in Christ Jesus.

<u>Focus On What You Believe</u>
Focus on reading the Word of God. Meditate on God's Word from the Bible.

Speak the Word of God out loud. Only confess the Word of God.

Align your thoughts, speech, and actions with what you believe, which is anchored in the Word of God.

Let your emotions be guided by your core beliefs. Let your beliefs be guided by the Word and promises of God.

Focus on psalms, hymns, and spiritual songs. Engage in worship, singing, and praise.

Make time to spend with God and Jesus by experiencing their loving and peaceful presence and engaging in conversation, fellowship, prayer, and praying in tongues.

<u>Fill the Void</u>
Make having a personal relationship with God your number one priority.

Only Jesus can fill your void and emptiness. Only God and Jesus can make you feel perfectly and unconditionally loved, worthy, and not condemned. Focus on your righteous identity in Christ, which you have received freely by the abundant grace of God.

Let your spoken words, thoughts, self-talk, and behavior reflect what is written in God's Word about your reconciliation with God, salvation, identity, and worth in Christ by grace. Let no words of defeat, despair, hopelessness, condemnation, and low self-worth cross your lips or thoughts unchecked. Immediately correct them if they do occur, by quoting the Word of God and reflecting on God's Word about who you are and your new life in Christ. Focus on Jesus.

Seek God and Jesus' presence each day. Seek to spend intimate, personal time with God and Jesus. Let their love and presence fill the void and emptiness versus seeking others and pleasures of the flesh.

Enter into fully resting in Christ by enjoying His peace and functioning by depending on Him to guide, lead, protect, provide for, and help you. Don't try to do it by your efforts, wisdom, and plans. Depend on Jesus.

Remember you are now a beloved child of God. He is your loving Abba Father.

Call on God and Jesus when you feel lonely, unworthy, and unloved, or when you feel desire and need or are tempted.

Pray in the Spirit (tongues) to directly communicate with God and to be edified and built up.

Recall, your body is the temple of the Holy Spirit. Remember to honor and respect your holy temple (your body). Look at yourself and see the righteousness of God in you, which you have received through Jesus. Look at yourself and see your holy temple, which contains God's Spirit. Look at yourself and recall you are loved by God, equally with Jesus. Look at yourself and see the glory of God in you.

Call out to Jesus in times of trouble and need, saying, "Merciful Savior, have mercy on me. Please help me. Please come."

Prayer

Pray in the Spirit (in tongues) at all times in every prayer and supplication.

Pray the Prayer of Protection (Psalm 91) to feel the presence of the Lord's peace in the middle of daily life as well as difficult, challenging, and dangerous times. Activate your angels into action by doing so. Also, pray this prayer and recall your privilege of being protected at all times, no matter what. Pray this prayer for your loved ones also.

Pray prayers of thanksgiving and praise to God.

Make your requests known unto God. Be open and honest. Believe that you receive in faith.

When you pray, focus on themes such as shame, unworthiness, guilt, condemnation, self-punishment, self-effort, choices, decisions you need to make, regret, loneliness, grief, loss, disappointments, need for wisdom, need for guidance, need for love, emotional pain and distress, disorders, sickness, hurt, sadness, letting go, anger, need for hope, comfort, empathy, acceptance, forgiveness, strength, guidance, struggles with your flesh, need, desire, lust, want, impulsiveness, and condemnation, need for a sense of purpose, lack of family and community, feeling empty, and following the will of God.

Focus on the promises of God toward you. Ask God to receive His many blessings and favor in your life. Ask for the desires of your heart and believe you will receive them, knowing that God is willing and able.

Pray for wisdom and discernment.

Pray for help from Jesus. Also, pray for intercession on your behalf by Jesus.

Following the Will of God

Focus on God's love for you and His mercy.

Ask Jesus to guide you and follow His lead. Let Jesus help you to do the will of God by resting in Him and being guided, shielded, and benefitting from His ever-present help.

In times of need, confusion, difficulties, seeking wisdom and direction, and in making choices, ask Jesus for help. He is your good shepherd.

Pray in the Spirit (in tongues).

Renew your mind to know the good, acceptable, and perfect will of God for your life.

Remember that by grace you have received the righteousness of God through Christ and are therefore entitled to the undeserved and overflowing blessings and favor of God, through Christ Jesus. You are a joint heir with Christ. None of it depends on what you deserve, but rather on what Jesus deserves. You are blessed freely by grace through Him. Simply activate it all by faith that Christ died for you.

Recall the promises of God are to do you no harm and to give you hope and a good future. Therefore, you can trust that God's will for you is best.

Renew Your Mind

Remember that God did not give you a spirit of fear, but of power, and of love and of a sound mind (2 Timothy 1:7).

Put on the whole armor of God to be able to stand your ground against the devil's schemes in spiritual warfare and in the battle for your mind.

Pray in the Spirit (in tongues) at all times in every prayer and supplication, being assured you will be edified and be in direct communication with God.

Take up the sword of the Spirit, which is the Word of God. Anchor yourself in the Word of God and make this your focus. Quote the scriptures when facing difficulties and as a confession of faith. Speak the Word of God into every situation you are facing. Say, "It is written," as Jesus did, and then quote whatever scripture pertains to your circumstance.

Take up the shield of faith with which you will quench all the fiery arrows, mind games, lies, and spiritual attacks of the devil. Focus on scriptures and on speaking and hearing the Word of God.

Put on the breastplate of righteousness. Focus on being righteous, forever, through Christ, who took all your sins and gave you the righteousness of God, not because of what you did, deserved, or must maintain, but based on the grace of God. It is a free gift by grace.

Focus on the truth (the belt of truth around your waist) in Christ and God, your Abba Father, who loves you. Defeat doubts and fears by saying, "I believe God and His truth."

Stand on the solid, stable, and safe ground of the gospel of peace, which you have received through Christ, by putting on the gospel of peace as shoes for your feet. Stand firm, knowing you can rest in His peace.

Place the helmet of salvation on your head, making sure you always focus your thoughts, beliefs, personal reflections, and spoken words on the life you have received through the sacrifice of Christ Jesus for you, your resurrection with Christ, your justification through Christ, your righteousness and identity in

Christ, your reconciliation with God, and the richness of the life to come. Focus on your eternal life in Christ. Also, focus on the love and grace of God, which made this possible.

Boldly declare the Word of God when you pray and when you speak.

Read Psalm 91 (the prayer of protection), declare it over yourself and your loved ones, focusing on being protected because of your relationship with Christ, and making your relationship and spiritual intimacy with God and Jesus the priority in your life. Focus on the love and grace of God, which makes this possible.

Believe and, therefore, speak what you believe as a saved child of God by the grace and faith that are in Christ Jesus.

Focus your mind on Christ, your Merciful Savior, as you bring every thought into submission. Christ Jesus is your good shepherd who helps you and guides you. He is your intercessor and High Priest. He is your strength. Rest in Him. He is your partner in helping you through life's difficulties. He is your Lord and Savior, who loves you and paid the price for your sins. By grace, let Him accomplish it all for you. Wait on the Lord and let Him renew your strength, to mount up with wings like eagles, run and not be weary, and walk and not faint (Isaiah 40:31). Rely on Jesus to fight your battles, follow God's will, and to be obedient and capable, all by grace.

Focus on God's unconditional love for you. Draw closer to Him and experience His perfect love. His love makes you feel worthy, whole, healed, valued, cared for, comforted, accepted, understood, and forgiven. Experience the truth of who God is and how much He compassionately loves you in a personal relationship with Him.

Focus your thoughts on the victory you have received already through Christ over everything you presently face or fear facing in the future. Focus on the fact that nothing you face is greater than what Christ already accomplished and what you have attained through being one with Christ. Praise God even when things seem too much to bear.

Focus on and think about whatsoever things are true, honest, honorable, just, pure, pleasing and of good report, commendable, lovely, things of virtue, and whatever is praiseworthy.

Pray prayers of thanksgiving and be grateful for every blessing. Look for the grace and the blessings of God in your life each day. Have an attitude of gratitude.

Focus on psalms, hymns, and spiritual songs. Sing spiritual songs. Sing in the Spirit.

Focus your thoughts on the promises of God, His plans to bless you and do you no harm, and to give you a good future, full of hope and every blessing, in Christ. Know that in Christ the promises of God are, "Yes," and in Christ Jesus you can say, "Amen."

Focus on being a righteous and holy temple of the Holy Spirit.

Enjoy the peace that comes from the presence of Christ and the Father.

Focus on loving one another, as God wants us to.

Remember the True Nature of God
God is love

God is loving, gracious, kind, compassionate, generous, giving, forgiving, merciful, faithful, good, protective, caring, comforting, understanding, empathetic, patient, attentive, and protective.

God is your loving Father, through Christ.
God is faithful.

Operate in Faith
God loves you.
Believe God, then confess with your mouth what you believe.

Trust God. He did not spare His own Son, Jesus, to save you, therefore He has proven He loves you and wishes the best for you. God is trustworthy.

Anchor yourself in your core beliefs, based on the Word of God. His Word proves true (Psalm 30:18).

Avoid continuously questioning everything and needing to know every detail of God's plans for your life.

Allow Jesus to be your good shepherd and lead you step by step.

Consider this. If God did not withhold His own Son to save you, what else would He not do for you?

Remember that Jesus is the originator and finisher of your faith. Ask Jesus to help you.

Listen to the Word of God. Faith comes by hearing the Word of God.

Don't Isolate
Ask God for help with establishing relationships with other children of God. Ask God for help in love and marriage.

Surround yourself with positive people of faith and belief in Christ, who believe in the grace, mercy, and love of God, that are in Christ. Let go of your past and old patterns that harmed you. Move forward.

Seek wise, Godly counsel. Seek a community of faith. Let Christ Jesus lead the way. Simply follow His guidance.

Trust God to provide who is best for you. Be guided by Jesus and the Holy Spirit.

Avoid negative and worldly people when forming intimate bonds.

Avoid seeking fulfillment, self-worth, and getting your needs and desires met in your relationships.

Be patient. Hope.

Love
Love is patient, kind, compassionate, not envious, not boastful or arrogant, not disrespectful or rude, not selfish or insisting on its own way, not irritable, not angry, not resentful; it is honest, tells the truth, does not hide, endures all things, and supports each other through difficulties and good times. Love forgives and is gracious and appreciative.

Love is the greatest of all the gifts.

Love one another.

Today's Powerful Thought
All praise and glory to my Abba Father
and my Lord and merciful Savior, Jesus.
God loves me and is gracious to me.

Prayer

Abba Father, thank You for loving me and for the grace and blessing I have received through the sacrifice of Jesus for my sins. Jesus, as my merciful Savior and good shepherd, I ask You to help me. By grace, I rest in You and rely on You. When facing difficulties and challenges, help me to rest in You, Jesus, and Your finished work on the cross. In the name of Jesus, I pray. Amen.

DAY 34

SCAVENGER HUNT FOR LOVE

God yearns jealously for the spirit that He has made to dwell in us. But He gives all the more grace.
—James 4:5–6

God loves us, His children, and yearns to favor His people. You must therefore believe that the miracle will happen. However, when you ask and do not receive, do not say it is because God withholds His favor. If you ask out of the desires of your fleshly pleasures and need, then consider that you may be asking wrongly (James 4:1–4). Love is something everyone wants to receive. The question is, "Why do you want a mate?"

Often, what people are searching for comes from an insatiable thirst, desire, and craving for a constant supply of love, validation, worthiness, acceptance, value, fulfillment, satisfaction, support, safety, protection, security, compassion, understanding, kindness, hopefulness, powerfulness, strength, and meaning.

People also seek to feel capable, alive, and purposeful. Many want a mate to fill the void and emptiness they feel inside.

What you have been searching for cannot supply these needs. Even a mate, who is a gift from God, can never be what you need. If you try to get your needs fulfilled in your human relationship with a mate, you will never be satisfied. What will result is a codependent, symbiotic, unhealthy relationship that functions on the level of need, desire, selfishness, emptiness, dissatisfaction, longing, resentment, and emotional turmoil. Even if you get married to a man who loves you as God intends, you will find that you still suffer from emptiness, unhappiness, and disappointment. As loving as your partner is, you may sabotage the relationship if it is reduced to functioning on the level of satisfying your desires and needs. Ultimately, you may still feel unworthy and unloved, despite how much your partner loves you.

God has provided the answer for what you need. You need not continue your search for love, worth, value, wholeness, protection, and peace. No one else but God can supply all the things you have been searching for in someone else. He provided the answer through offering you a personal relationship with His Son, Jesus, and Himself. To state it more plainly, your desire to get married must never become the focus of your every waking thought and action. You must not allow your actions and emotions to be driven and manipulated by your desire for a mate. You will never experience a sense of fulfillment of all you are seeking in a relationship with a mate. It is not your solution.

The gift of love from Abba Father is absolutely better and more fulfilling and complete. The perfect, unconditional love of the Father and your spiritual relationship with Him and Christ Jesus are the only things that will heal your hurt and make you whole. A relationship with God must become the priority and central focus of your life. God intended this so that you would no longer suffer. God is the one you absolutely need. Through His Son, Jesus, He provided a way to save you and make you righteous, justified, holy, healed, whole, and reconciled with Himself, by grace. All you are required to do is believe by faith. Once you do, you become one with Jesus and the Father, God. This is what gives you the fulfillment you have been seeking. Jesus is the only man you need. This is why God yearns for us to come to Him and be back in relationship with Him, so that we can be saved and made whole by grace, through Jesus, and be reconciled with Himself.

Yes, love from a mate is a beautiful blessing and gift to your life. You should pray and ask to receive this gift if you want to share your life with a mate. However, unconditional love and all the other things you have been seeking will only be guaranteed and attained in your personal relationship with God, the Father, and Jesus, your Lord and Savior. There is no substitute for God and Jesus in your life. A husband cannot become your substitute Savior. It is essential you not expect your mate to fulfill the roles of God and Jesus in your life, and give you the kind of love, validation, identity, value, wholeness, completion, fulfillment, compassion, support, understanding, empathy, happiness, safety, protection, security, meaning, sense of purpose, and strength that only your relationship with God and Jesus can provide. In Jesus, your salvation, righteousness, and core identity as a beloved, blessed, and favored child of God, and joint heir with Him (Christ) are established. No mate can ever do this for you.

Today, take some time to spend with God and Jesus. Enjoy the gift of truly receiving God's perfect love. Spend time just soaking in

His unconditional love for you. Talk freely and openly without holding back. Experience His mercy and grace. God earnestly yearns to spend time with you, and He is always gracious and welcoming (James 4:5–6). God is your Father who loves you. Make this your priority today and each day. When you turn your heart in the right direction, all other things will be added to you (Matthew 6:32–33).

Today's Powerful Thought
I am important to my Father, God. I will find everything I need in a relationship with Him and my Lord and Savior, Jesus.

Prayer
Father, You are God, the Most High, the powerful creator and my loving Abba Father. Thank You that You gave me Jesus as my Savior and offered me grace and mercy. Thank You that You satisfy all my needs. Thank You that I will never be disappointed when I turn to You. Thank You, Jesus, for loving me and being my Lord and Savior. Praise to You, Father, for providing me the ultimate gift of perfect love, healing, hope, and a new life, through the sacrifice of Your own Son, Jesus, by Your grace. Please help me to be healed and whole in my relationship with You. In the name of Jesus, I pray. Amen.

DAY 35

LEARNING TO LOVE

You have received the gift of love. It is not based on how good you are or whether you deserve it. Likewise, we are asked to love each other as Christ loves us (John 15:12). However, admittedly, this is a challenge. In learning to love, you will need to be patient and endure. It takes commitment, stamina, and practice. You are asked to be patient, kind, compassionate, not envious, not arrogant, not boastful, not disrespectful, not selfish, not insisting on your own way, not irritable, not angry, not resentful, not crafty, and not deceitful (1 Corinthians 13:1). What this suggests is that in love, there must be real affection and genuine deeper feelings.

Love is not reflected in being right or getting the last word in, even when your mate is wrong or has hurt you. Love asks you to forgive and step away from pursuing a disagreement or saying harsh words that wound the other. After all, what will the unfortunate payoff be in wounding the other? Learning to love means acting in love at all times, with deepest loving intention. It never compromises. This is the way Jesus loves us, His bride.

When you personally experience the compassion, grace, forgiveness, acceptance, healing, and wholeness offered by God's love, you will find it is easier to more fully and genuinely love another as well. This is because you will have the perfect love that fulfills your needs. Anchored in God's love, your broken heart will be healed, and you will find you are better able to love and appreciate another with patience and endurance, even during difficult times or times when you are deeply wounded by your mate or he is not acting lovingly toward you. God's love offers the very special gift of forgiveness and grace. Through receiving this gift from God, you will learn to forgive and offer grace, mercy, compassion, empathy, acceptance, and understanding to your mate and others. This offers the opportunity to fall more deeply and richly in mutual love with each other.

Love is patient, which is of particular value and benefit. Being patient in love means allowing yourself to wait and make the choice to voluntarily and lovingly respond with compassion, understanding, and forgiveness, instead of reacting on impulse, need, and raw emotion. In being patient, there is also an absence of rushing to judgment, condemnation, vengefulness, and anger. Being patient allows for the natural, respectful, and sensitive unfolding of mutual understanding and consideration of each other's perspectives, personal histories, struggles, and needs.

Eventually, this leads to mutual compassion, forgiveness, and the flow of continuous positive affection and engagement between you and the one you love. Patience in love says, "I believe in the quality of our love and the union between us, which God has blessed, and so I will exercise patience as we learn to love each other more—like the way Christ and our Father teaches us to love one another." When you love each other, exercising patience will help you both stay the course and go through the long journey together, no matter how many twists, turns, and obstacles come up ahead. Your love story endures.

Love is a gift to both yourself and the other. It means going through life's problems and journey over time together. It perseveres. Love keeps asking you to go deeper and to love more. Love says, "All I know to do is love you more." The more you love, the more you love even more. It is a beautiful connection of mutual empathy, commitment, faithfulness, understanding, forgiveness, and acceptance. Love creates the space to be who you really are, without judgment and fear. Love allows for and facilitates changing, learning, growing, and maturing together. Love instrumentally helps you to endure misfortunes and suffering in life as a couple. It also strengthens you and provides a protective buffer of support and compassion, which helps you to overcome the challenges of life.

Positively, love alleviates suffering. Love is solid, dependable, and does not yield. This points to the reassurance that love with another will bear all things. This includes bearing disappointments, problems, and life transitions that you will go through over the course of your lives. Being dependable and solid, despite how difficult and painful it gets, love never ends. It does not transfer to another person. You both remain constant and faithful.

There is hopefulness in love. The experience of love is hopeful. Love called you to a new life in Christ and reconciliation with God. God's love healed you and made you whole. God's love ignites hopefulness for better days and the promise of experiencing a good life. It offers you the opportunity to first believe and then, with gratitude, passionately and fully embrace life on the deepest level possible. As you grow in maturity, you will experience the fruitfulness of love and how naturally it connects you to others and the beauty of life and love of another.

Love strengthens you and helps you to be better. You are called to be of good courage and to wait on the Lord to strengthen your heart (Psalms 27:14). In the matter of love, this is especially critical. In the process of waiting for love with a mate, take the opportunity to grow deeper in love in your connection with the Lord. Benefit from the experience of His love for you. Fully embrace this experience. The journey of love is both beautiful and challenging, even when you feel the deepest, most genuine love possible. Remember, you will always need God's love to sustain you. He offers you the perfect love you seek. The love He offers will also help you to act with more loving intention when you eventually are blessed with a loving relationship with a mate.

Recall to yourself often these things and speak them out loud. "I have the love of my merciful Savior, who died for me on the cross. I have the love of my Father, who shows me compassion and forgiveness. I am a beloved child of God and have received hope and a future."

Today's Powerful Thought
How beautiful is love, which I receive as a child of God.

Prayer
Abba Father, help me to grow deeper in love and to experience all the deeply layered, beautiful qualities of love. Have mercy on me as I try to honor the love

I receive and to offer love more like the love I have already received from You and Jesus. Please strengthen me as I await the miracle of love in my life with a mate. Bless our union and help us to love with loving intention, in the way You ask us to love one another. Help me when I struggle with being loving, fear loving someone and accepting love, experience anxiety, or impatience, and am scared of letting go of my past. Help me to move forward in the strength of Your Spirit to love and experience the gift of love in a relationship with another. Help me to be guided by You and to always walk in Your will and way. Help me to not be critical, harsh, argumentative, angry, judgmental, and punitive, but to instead show compassion and forgive. Help me to remain positive and to place my trust and hope in You and Your Word, promises of love, and all Your blessings for my life. May it all be fulfilled in Your perfect time. I believe. In the name of Jesus, I pray. Amen.

NOTES

1. Retrieved March 23, 2021, from https://hebrew4christians.com/Names_of_G-d/El/el.html
2. St John of Tobolsk, Translated from Russian by Nicholas Kotar, *The Sunflower: Conforming the Will of Man to the Will of God* (Holy Trinity Publications, NY, 2018).

ABOUT THE AUTHOR

Dr. Evelyn Jagpat is a Christian clinical psychologist, spiritual and relationship coach, author, poet, mentor, and an expert in love and relationships, trauma, and integrating spiritual and psychological practices—all based on the written Word of God. She offers national online telehealth therapy and professional coaching services, with an emphasis on love, relationships, healing from a broken heart, and various spiritual and mental health issues. Dr. Jagpat has a YouTube channel dedicated to love, relationships, and teaching how to apply practical spiritual and psychological strategies when facing challenges in love, relationships, and everyday life. She also focuses on helping others to connect with the love of the Lord and God in practical ways that promote healing, emotional health, and love.

She believes it is important to honor all aspects of self in the healing process. Her approach to treatment integrates spiritual and psychological practices so one can enjoy the experience of becoming more deeply spiritual and human in harmony. She focuses on practical spiritual and psychological strategies for resolving problems related to relationships, love, and mental health issues, while navigating spiritual growth in the real world, coping with life transitions, negotiating milestones and stages of growth and development, and facing everyday challenges and life in general. She believes in the importance of integrating God's love and grace in one's personal narrative, identity, beliefs, thoughts, words, and actions. She recognizes the powerful impact of aligning your thoughts and actions intentionally with God's Word to thrive. She is also an expert in helping others develop a healthy core identity and sense of worth based on the foundations of love, grace, and righteousness received through Christ and being reconciled with God as a beloved child of God.

Further, Dr. Jagpat helps others navigate the difficult challenges of love and relationships and the conflicts, temptations, and struggles they face when trying to integrate their spiritual beliefs in the real world of love, dating, seeking a partner, and marriage. You can find out more by connecting with her online and via social media.

STAY CONNECTED

YouTube.com (Evelyn Jagpat)
EvelynJagpat.com
CATSSaustin.com
Twitter.com/IamDrEve
Instagram@iamdreve

Made in the USA
Coppell, TX
20 July 2021